THE FRUGAL TRAVELER

Other books by Marion Joyce

The Coupon Cookbook

The Frugal Shopper

THE
FRUGAL
TRAVELER

MARION JOYCE

A PERIGEE BOOK

Perigee Books
are published by
The Putnam Publishing Group
200 Madison Avenue
New York, NY 10016

"The Frugal Traveler is a trademark belonging to Marion Joyce"

Library of Congress Cataloging-in-Publication Data

Joyce, Marion.
The frugal traveler.

"A Perigee book."
1. Travel. I. Title.
G151.J68   1987   910'.2'02   87-7281
ISBN 0-399-51409-0

Printed in the United States of America
1   2   3   4   5   6   7   8   9   10

Disclaimers

Neither the author nor the publisher make any representations or guarantees as to the products, services, prices or other information described in this book, due to the constantly changing nature of the travel industry. All coupons in this book are void where prohibited, taxed or restricted by law.

Many of the trademarks in this book are registered with the U.S. Patent and Trademark Office and may not be used without permission.

Author and publisher are NOT responsible for company coupon offers, or for withdrawal or changes of offers. Unauthorized reproduction of coupons is illegal.

To Leo, Pamela, and Lisa,
my traveling companions through life.
Always
Seek
Knowledge

Acknowledgments

I wish to thank the participating products and companies for their generosity in providing redeemable coupons for the products and services found in this book. See pages 000 to 000.

To the reader: Clip the coupons and enjoy thousands of dollars of savings!

Company	*Product/Service*
Air New Zealand	Airline Flights
American Museum Hayden Planetarium	Admission
Arizona Jeep Tours	Jeep Tours, Scottsdale, AZ
Bed & Breakfast	Accommodations
Best Western Red Jacket Inn	Hotel Accommodations, Niagara Falls, NY
Budget	Car and Truck Rental
Captains Corner	Excursions, Key West, FL
Caribbean Express	Airline Flights
Caribbean Yacht Charters, Inc.	Caribbean Sailing
Comprehensive Communications Inc.	Video Tapes
Comprehensive Communications Inc.	Audio Tape Touring
Discount Travel International	Travel Club
Edison Theater	*Oh! Calcutta!* Theater Tickets, NYC
Empire State Building	Observatory Admission
Entertainment Publications, Inc.	Club Express Membership
Entertainment Publications, Inc.	Travel, Hotel and Condo
Executive Lodge	Hotel Accommodations, Santa Ana, CA
Firestone	Transmission Service
Firestone	Premium Brake Service
Firestone	Lube, Oil and Filter
Firestone	Air Conditioning Service
Firestone	Supreme Battery
Fotomat	Film
Fotomat	Developing
Fotomat	Poster Prints
Frugal Shopper	Frugal Shopper Newsletter discount
Gessler Publishing Co., Inc.	Video Language Instruction
Gessler Publishing Co., Inc.	Foreign Language Games
Gessler Publishing Co., Inc.	Foreign Language Software
The Great Gorge Resort	Resort Accommodations
The Gray Line Co.	Tours of New York City
The Gray Line Co.	Tours of Hoover Dam & Las Vegas

Guinness World Records	Exhibit Hall Admissions
Ha' Penny Inn	Hotel, El Cajon, CA
Ha' Penny Inn	Hotel, Huntington Beach, CA
Ha' Penny Inn	Hotel, National City, CA
Ha' Penny Inn	Hotel, Westminster, CA
Kittatinny Campgrounds	Camping, Barryville, NY
Kittatinny Canoes	Delaware River Canoe and Raft Trips
Manhattan Helicopter Tours	Helicopter Tours
Marriott	Hotel, Newark Airport, NJ
Moment's Notice	Travel Club
Ocean Key House	Hotel and Marina, Key West, FL
Payless Car Rental	Car Rental
The Pierre	Hotel, Weekend Package, NYC
Pines Hotel	Hotel, South Fallsburg, NY
Quality Inn	Hotel, Ontario, CA
Ramada	Ramada Best Years Program for Seniors
Ramada	Ramada Supersaver Weekend
River Beach Campsites	Camping, Milford, PA
Russel's	Dining, New York City's East Side
Sardi's	Dining, New York City's Theater District
Sears	Car and Truck Rental
Sheraton Stamford Hotel & Towers	Weekend Getaway
Sheraton Stamford Hotel & Towers	Romance Package
Sheraton Stamford Hotel & Towers	Weekend Special
South Florida Cruises	All Major Cruise Lines
Stand-Buys Ltd.	Travel Club Membership
Steve Colgate's Offshore Sailing School Ltd.	Sailing Instruction
Stouffer Hotels	Club Express Membership
Stouffer Hotels	Hotel Room Upgrade
Superior Rent-a-Car	Car Rental (1st time)
Superior Rent-a-Car	Car Rental (2nd time)
Unicorn Balloon Company of Colorado	Balloon Flights, Aspen, CO
Unicorn Balloon Company of Arizona	Balloon Flights, Scottsdale, AZ
Unicorn Balloon Company of Arizona	T-Shirt
Valef Yachts Ltd.	Luxury Yachts, Greece
Waterfront Airways	Airline Flights
Waterfront Airways	Airline Flights
Wilson World	Hotel, Disney World, Epcot Center, FL
Worldwide Discount Travel Club	Travel Club
The Y's Way	Travel Catalog

Contents

Introduction

I travel. I have been traveling for years, all the while making a study of travel trials and tribulations. I have examined lodging facilities of all styles, sizes, and purposes—from the small country inn, mountain top cabin and chateau, to enormous contemporary convention complexes—from lavish resorts to quaint, romantic hideaways, and spas, sports camps, and family run bed-and-breakfast inns and guest houses.

I've studied what makes good travel value for business travelers, and what is necessary to give the best value to pleasure-seeking vacationers.

This book is all about sharing with you how to get the best values, how to eliminate troubles and frustrations, and how to have the best, the least stressful, easiest, most successful trip possible—from the time you start planning your trip until you get back home where you started from.

As a consumer advisor and nationally syndicated newspaper columnist, I travel throughout the US, appearing on radio and television shows, and over the years I've found I get more questions from the public about travel than about any other topic.

But it wasn't until readers of my newspaper column, "Consumer Corner," as well as my radio listeners and television viewers, told me again and again that they needed some basic information on getting the best travel value for their dollar that I knew I had to write *The Frugal Traveler*.

Not too many years ago only the rich and top business executives traveled extensively. Today, most people travel, and today's traveler is faced with an extraordinarily vast range of choices. The travel industry, and the other industries that service travelers—from telephone services to credit cards—have been changing at such a fast rate that contemporary traveling consumers often experience confusion when selecting the best travel package or making the right travel arrangements to fit their needs, desires and budgets.

Other travel books will give you specific recommendations for travel to various locations, but the very people who write these travel guides are often the first to admit that, by the time a given guidebook is published, much of its information is obsolete. *The Frugal Traveler,* on the other hand, is a general overview of the greatest travel values, and how to find them. This information is for travelers of every spending level, from the richest of the rich to those who must watch every penny. *The Frugal Traveler* gives solid and practical travel information—advice that will be helpful for many years—and tips useful for both the novice and the experienced traveler, the business person as well as the vacationer. Whether on a limited budget, trying to get the most out of a business trip, or seeking a luxurious holiday, everyone wants to get the best value possible—and *The Frugal Traveler* is here to help. Armed with the knowledge of the travel business contained in the following pages you will spend less—and enjoy more—on your next vacation or business trip—and on all your travels.

• 1 •

The

Frugal Traveler

Travels In Style

The Frugal Traveler always saves money by finding the best values. Sometimes the best value is not the lowest price, so you have to compare the prices and what is included for that price to ascertain the best value. Understand that the *best value* is the bargain that the Frugal Traveler seeks, not necessarily the cheapest price. Many of the world's richest people are Frugal Travelers, even though saving money is not their goal. Their goal, however, as yours should be, is to get the best value for the money they are spending, even though they will be spending more than a person with budget limits. The big difference is that, as your money supply dwindles, you have fewer choices. Nevertheless, there are, at any budget level, good values to be found throughout the world.

You can travel like a millionaire by finding luxury vacations at bargain prices. To get the best buys on all your travel needs, you must find the right discount travel groups and clubs, and the best ways to pay for travel expenses that will save you money. Check directly with airlines for their packages, which may be good buys. To get the very cheapest prices, however, you may need to use bucket or charter operators and coupon discounters. You really can afford the vacation of your dreams, the one you thought was beyond your means, but you must, if your funds are limited, save money by knowing how to get those bargains.

DISCOVERING THE BASICS— THE VALUE OF PLANNING

Americans spend billions of dollars each year traveling. This spending power should "put you in the driver's seat" for finding excellent travel values. Wherever you decide to go, *good planning* is perhaps the single most important factor in making a vacation or business trip a success. Proper planning requires that before you take your trip you play detective and seek information. This really pays off if you learn about the options available to you, how to get the most out of your trip and how to avoid difficulties. Planning includes taking steps—such as taking out certain insurance policies before your trip—to avoid the catastrophic expenses, which can result from emergencies. It also means knowing what to do if you run into problems. This book is designed to assist you in finding out all you can during your travel-planning stage. You may save hundreds to thousands of dollars per trip if you use the information in this book and follow some of my suggestions while investigating and planning your trip. This proper planning is the best assurance that you will get the best value for the money you spend both for and during your trip.

As you will discover, there are many fantastic money-saving opportunities available for every type of trip, from deluxe to budget. You will discover that you may only be able to obtain or qualify for certain excellent opportunities if you plan and arrange for them some time in advance of your departure. Planning also helps eliminate many of the hassles and problems of travel, both during transit and once you have arrived at your destination. Become a Frugal Traveler, an educated consumer, and get more for your money by knowing the "ins" and "outs" of the travel industry, where and how to find the bargains and other valuable information for luxury or basic travel. The Frugal Traveler can travel in high style for bargain prices. Read on, and find out how.

PLANNING YOUR TRIP: SHOULD YOU USE A TRAVEL AGENT?

In planning your trip one of the first questions you should consider is whether it is to your benefit to hire a professional travel agent, or whether you are better off planning your trip yourself. To make a wise decision you will need to know what a travel agent can and cannot do for you, and how to select an agent. You must first find the right agency and then find out which agent in that agency really knows and cares enough to give you the best information and make the best arrangements for you. This entails knowing the types of travel agencies and travel clubs and organizations, and the types of discounts, coupons and rebates available for business and vacation travel. A knowledgeable Frugal Traveler knows how to recognize a real bargain, and how to take advantage of it. Even if you do decide on a travel agent, you must still do a certain amount of planning on your own, and the following information should help you work with an agent or by yourself, whichever you decide is best for you.

THE TRAVEL AGENT

First, it is important for you to know what a travel agent should, can, and cannot do for you, so you will be able to tell if an agent is really doing the job.

You have the right to expect an agent to have firsthand knowledge of a wide range of destinations, especially the one he or she may be telling you to go to, and of the tour operators and carriers they recommend. Travel agents who charge full commission on travel services should earn their commission by giving a great deal of personal attention to their clients' travel planning.

Experienced travelers expect their agents to obtain the lowest prices generally available in the marketplace, which include the discount prices. Frugal Travelers look for an agency that is likely to find them the best deals, using the guidelines the traveler sets. If discounts interest you most, find the type of discount agency that best suits your needs and then look for a specific one in a convenient location close to you.

In today's travel world, many ordinary agencies—large and small—have adapted themselves to today's marketplace and have access to most discount cost-cutting opportunities. Make sure your agency can and is willing to obtain discount international airline tickets from a consolidator, coupons from a broker or discount cruises from a cruise line or clearing house, if you can use these discounts. Even a small, independent, but active and modern agency can obtain many discount travel services for you.

Tip: If you check out prices in your town and those in a bigger city, you may find you can save a great deal of money if you use an agency in a nearby larger city with a more competitive market than you can in your home town, even though it may entail some inconvenience and additional expenses.

You should decide what kind of agent you need—a full-service travel agent or one simply to execute the arrangements you specify. Some agencies will pass savings on to you if you do the work and they merely book reservations for you. If you decide you need a full-service agent, choose one based on the kind of expertise you require. There are specialists in every type of travel.

Over the years I have discovered that one of the best ways to find a good agent is through references from friends, relatives, and business associates—especially those who are in a similar spending bracket as you. You can sometimes find the right travel agency by looking in the Sunday travel section of your local newspaper, or in the phone book for travel agents specializing in a particular type of travel. But no matter how you find the agent, interview him or her. And keep in mind that unless there is a good one with up-to-date computer equipment in your area, it is best to use an agent that is near to where you live or work.

Before you hire, make sure your travel agent is a member of a professional travel agents' association. Check with the Better Business Bureau for any prior complaint records. You should also ask for—and check—references from other clients.

You should be able to depend on an agent to make all or most of your travel arrangements, including all reservations during the trip. Your agent must be able to set up individual itineraries and make arrangements for group-package tours or personally escorted tours, finding the best deal available for whatever you want. You need to be able to rely on this agent for important up-to-the-minute information on vital details such as political unrest, special travel situations, the current conditions of hotels, luggage and medical insurance, visas, passports, innoculations, traveler's checks, currency exchange, weather conditions, a practical wardrobe, travel budgeting and whatever special interests you may have.

When you use a travel agent, you have every right to assume that the transportation, accommodations and any package you purchase will be exactly as it was represented. For example, if you were led to believe that your accommodations were on or near the beach, and you find that they are not, you need to have recourse to hold the travel agent responsible. Find an agency that has been in business for a long time and will stand behind what it says.

SOME THINGS TO WATCH FOR

It is standard practice for travel agents to be paid by airlines, steamship lines, rental companies, railroads, hotels and resorts and tour operators, in the form of commissions. Be wary of an agent sending you on a more expensive trip just because the agent gets a better commission or some other reward or bonus for that booking. And you should be aware of the fact that you may be charged for such extras as special telegrams, long-distance telphone calls, reticketing, making reservations in certain hotels, short-stay hotel reservations and cancellations. And, if a travel agency or tour operator says they will make refunds for cancellations you may make for valid reasons, find out just what constitutes "valid reasons." Also, if a slight penalty is to be imposed in the event you cancel, check just how slight is "slight."

If the agent does not spend time with you and ask a lot of questions about your budget and your expectations for the trip, and if the agent does not know specifically about the area in which you will be traveling or the kind of trip you want—particularly if it is a specialized trip—look for another agent. Again, make sure that you understand what services are included as free and ask for specifics, in writing, of the fees for not-included services. Most of the services should be free.

You must be able to trust your agent with your valuable money. He or she is guiding you in spending from hundreds to thousands of dollars, and is largely responsible for setting up a successful trip. Your agent should sort out for you the constantly changing airfare, credit card, hotel and transportation come-on offers, misleading small-print advertising, potential airline and charter bankruptcies, mergers and restrictive clauses. It takes a lot of effort on the part of a travel agent to keep track of daily-changing world travel conditions, including the latest, cheapest and best airfares to fit your itinerary and budget. A good agent can often suggest minor changes in your trip that, through the use of special offerings, or slight itinerary changes, might save you hundreds or even thousands of dollars.

A good travel agent is a good deal. He or she is there to serve you, help you, guide and protect you and to save you work, time and money. A good agent will put together an itinerary just for you, and will make sure you have the right documents and insurance protections and will stand behind you if you do not get what you are entitled to on your trip. You can expect all this and more when you use the right travel agent for you, and all these services are usually free.

PLANNING YOUR TRIP:
THE FRUGAL TRAVELER IN ACTION

The individual who does not wish to use a travel agent needs to become more of an expert than the traveler who has decided to use an agent, but in my experience I've found that the lessons learned by the self-planned traveler are invaluable and forever helpful.

If you decide to plan your own trip, it is most important that you begin to prepare by doing the following. Even if you do decide to use an agent these things will be helpful.

- Study several travel guide books, which you can borrow from your library or buy at a bookstore. Get a feel for what is involved in the vacation you have in mind.
- Make sure you understand the travel terminology that appears in books and the brochures that interest you; it can sometimes be confusing, or written in a tricky way. Consider particularly the lines that appear in small print in brochures and travel contracts. You can consult a travel agent about travel terms or about the details of a trip or brochure even if you do not use that agency. They are used to shoppers, and accept it as part of their business.
- An important source for the most current travel offerings and special discounts is the Sunday travel section of your local newspaper; local radio and television stations as well as the local newspaper in the area of your travel destination can also be useful.
- Other current information can be found in travel magazines and specialty magazines for the areas or type of trip you are planning. Check into these.
- Tourist offices that represent your destination will also have general information about their area, and many also have current information about events and specific travel packages in their area.
- Travel brochures, of course, are an excellent source of information, but check to see if they are current and still have valid information.
- And last, but very important, word-of-mouth recommendations and travel tips from people you know who have taken the same or a similar trip can be the most important information you can get about a trip. Ask friends, relatives and business associates who have similar tastes and standards as yours about their travel arrangements. Learn about their positive and negative experiences and consider their tales in making your travel decisions.

PLANNING MAKES PERFECT

As you begin to make the vacation in your mind a reality, I have found the following useful in the day-by-day planning of a Frugal Traveler get-away:

- Toll-free 800-numbers, whenever available, can be used to call airlines, cruise lines, tourist departments, rental agencies, hotel and motel chains and others to investigate their latest promotional discount opportunities. (Call 1-800-555-1212 for the 800-numbers you need.)

You will be amazed that you will often not get the best price unless you ask specifically for the best price available to you. After you think you have the best price, hang up and call again, reaching another reservations operator. You may be further amazed when you get a better price this time. Do this a third time, and you may get even a better deal. Call back at a later date before your trip to see if there are any better promotional or even cheaper prices and ask if there are cancellation penalties for the deal. If not, or if the deal is so good you are willing to risk the penalty, pay with a credit card to hold the reservation.

Make sure you get your reservation number—you would be amazed how often your records and bargain deals can be lost by a computer. They can usually be traced if you have your reservation number. Always ask for a written confirmation of your reservation to avoid arriving at the hotel and having a bewildered clerk tell you there is no record of your discount or your reservation. If you are forced to cancel, or change your reservation in any way, get a written confirmation of this as well. And make sure you get the cancellation number before you hang up the phone. It also helps to get the operator's name when making any reservations or cancellations. Keep these records in case the written correspondence you have requested never gets to you, and record the dates and times of your calls.

- When you book a package, make sure the extras you are entitled to are included. You must *ask* about extras—often they forget to tell you everything you are entitled to. Recently a friend of mine stayed at an airport hotel and left his car parked in the airport parking lot. It cost him $40. The clerk at the airport hotel and the agent who booked the room forgot to tell him that parking at the hotel, for the duration of the trip, was included in his package.
- Call smaller businesses directly for transportation, enter-

tainment and lodgings to ask if they offer discounts. If you will be giving them a lot of business or if you will be staying at a small or medium size hotel for a week or more, ask for a discount. This is especially important if you are traveling to out-of-the-way places, or in off-peak slow times. You will be amazed at the number of unexpected bargains you can find if you ask for a better price, or ask for some extras at the regular price or even at the bargain price. The Frugal Traveler always asks!

Tip: Best advice. When planning your trip, don't be bashful. Ask questions. Ask for discounts as if there is a cheaper price. You often get it just for asking since there are so many promotions around. As you will discover in the final section of this chapter, asking is central to the money-saving plan I call the Frugal Traveler's $aving $ystem.

Remember, plan as far ahead as you can so you can get the widest selection of transportation and accommodations—except, of course, if you are going to use a discount travel club or other last-minute travel arrangement for getting a super bargain. See the coupon section at the back of this book for discounts on these clubs and hotels, which will be discussed later. The high-and-low-end reservations are usually filled the fastest. If you hear of a special discount, which seems to be just what you want, reserve it immediately; if it is a really good deal, there may be limited quantities available and it will be taken immediately by other Frugal Travelers.

THE LAST-MINUTE TRAVELER

If you do not care about saving money, or if you must take a trip at the last minute, you may discover an opening by calling a hotel or airline direct. You will usually pay full price for the trip when you make direct arrangements, and usually good value package rates will be closed to you. I would be remiss if I did not let you know that hotels will probably charge you rack rate, which is the standard quoted hotel price. Others may be staying at the same hotel—in a comparable room—at a discount that might be half of what you will pay. If you are going to an out-of-the-way place, however, and you think there may be many vacancies, you can bargain for a cheaper price. On a long airline flight the differences in fares for last-minute travelers could be many hundreds of dollars over what others in your seat-class are paying. Only a very few routes offer cheap stand-by fares.

But last-minute travelers can also use special travel discounters who handle only last-minute travel arrangements. They can sometimes save you from 20 to 80% on a trip, if they handle that itinerary. Frequently, during high-peak seasons, the last-minute discount travel agencies are the only resource for the last-minute traveler. The bargain hunter, and even the rich—no matter how much they are willing to pay—can find themselves in the lurch during high season if they have no advance reservations and there is no availability. The air-and-land-packages that discount agencies handle vary, from budget to luxury, and you sometimes find a real luxury-travel, last-minute opening for a truly budget price, which enables you to go to destinations and resorts that you always thought were far beyond your means—an exotic safari, for example, or a cruise around the Greek islands.

In order to deal with these discounters, you must know what you are doing. You need to be able to make up your mind quickly about an available trip, otherwise you will probably lose it. You must know about the value of the package being offered, and you must know if the specific hotel, airline space and destination being offered is what you want, and if the price quoted you is a good price. If you do not make up your mind on the spot, most of these deals are so good that if you call back later, the offer will be already taken by another Frugal Traveler.

You may have to join a club, and pay a fee to participate in these offers. Evaluate each club, its reputation and how long it has been in business. Call the Better Business Bureau to check on complaint records. If you use the clubs, the membership fees pay for themselves easily in the travel savings you get. Check that most of the trips of the particular club you join have departures from ports or airports close to your home. Do not join a club that usually has trips leaving from Boston if you live in Philadelphia or Chicago. The cost and inconvenience of the point of departure may offset any potential savings.

A knowledgable, educated consumer is best able to take advantage of discount travel clubs. In order to use these clubs the customer needs to be flexible, so that he or she can travel to one of the several openings offered on the date they become available. This flexibility can pay off magnificently with a wonderful trip at a fraction of the costs of booking in advance through a traditional travel agency.

TRAVEL TERMS

Before we go any further, I think it is necessary to become familiar with some basic travel terms. They will help you to understand what comes later, as we discuss different kinds of trips. And remember, if you have any further questions, call a local travel agent or major airline tour desk—it's part of their job.

HOTELS AND MEAL PLANS

Single Supplement: The amount you'll pay extra (for a hotel room or a car rental) if traveling alone.

Single: One person in a private room. There is usually a supplemental charge added to the single price, as most prices are based on double occupancy. Sometimes the supplement can go as high as 80%. *Ask!*

Double: Two persons sharing a room. Prices may be quoted for the room or per person—sometimes brochures are not clear about this. If not sure, always ask whether price quoted is for one or two people. Usually there is no charge for two beds. When meals are included, the price is usually on a per-person basis.

Suite: Parlor and one or more bedrooms. More and more hotels are offering suites for business travelers—particularly some chains—at prices close to that of a single room. Suites can include kitchen facilities, which make them ideal for families.

Triple: Third person in a room.

Reconfirm: A double check on reservations.

Rack Rate: Published tariff per day. Usually posted on the room door. Usually lower are tour rates, weekend rates in hotels catering to business travelers and midweek rates in many resorts.

HOTEL CLASSIFICATIONS

Ratings differ around the world and standards abroad often vary from those in the US. Economy hotels in many countries may not have rooms with private baths. A classification of first-class lodging varies—but most will likely have private baths and such services as dining rooms, room service and bellhops. In some countries, first class is very mediocre. A hotel with the highest levels of accommodations, service and decor is usually called deluxe. Some government tourist offices rate hotels with stars: five stars usually the highest. However, in some countries six or four stars can be highest. Know the rating in your destination. Classification terms may not reflect American standards.

Meal Plans: A daily hotel rate with breakfast and one or two other meals.

A La Carte: Each item of food ordered is charged separately.

American Plan (AP): Room and three meals per day are included, with prices usually quoted on a per-person basis.

Continental Plan (CP): Continental Breakfast: Breakfast is included in the price of the accommodations. The breakfast may be complete or a light meal.

European Plan (EP): Prices quoted are for accommodations—no meals are included.

Full American Plan (FAP) or full pension: With a complete breakfast, lunch and dinner.

Modified American Plan (MAP) or demipension: Room and two meals per day are included. In most instances, meals are breakfast and dinner. Prices are usually quoted on a per-person basis.

Table d'Hôtel or Fixed Price Meal (TDH, FP): Full meal for a set price, usually with no substitutions permitted.

Check-out Time: The time posted in your room beyond which you are obliged to pay for an additional stay. Sometimes, arrangements can be made with the hotel management if you need to stay in the room a couple of hours beyond check-out time. Usually you can arrange with management so there is no charge if the hotel isn't full, or if they don't need your room that day for an incoming guest.

On- and Off-Season (high and low season or peak- and off-peak season): On, high, or peak season is the period when the hotel or resort is busiest and most expensive. Off, low, or off-peak season is the slow period, when rooms usually cost less money.

TOURS

Independent Tour (IT): For travel on your own, or with friends or family, an IT offers freedom, flexibility and guaranteed prearranged rates for such basics as airfare, hotel and ground transportation. An example is a fly-drive program that provides unlimited mileage. This can combine specified airfare, and a waiting rental car and perhaps some hotel accommodation.

Group Inclusive Tour Fare (GIT): The group, assembled by a tour operator, may fly together at substantial savings, and then split up when the plane lands. Be sure to compare costs with other excursion fares, since the GIT may not always be the best deal.

Escorted Tour (ET): Travel with other people and be guided by a tour guide. Volume discounts on hotels, transportation and meals.

Foreign Independent Travel (FIT): An itinerary custom-made to your specifications by a travel agent. For complex routings and arrangements, expect a service charge.

Tour Group: Group purchased the same package trip arrangements but may or may not spend time together.

Public Charters: Advertised flights are open to all. Club membership or other eligibility requirements. Usually for a discounted package or airfare.

Promotional Fares: Discounted prices often having various restrictions. Examples are SuperSaver, on domestic flights, and the international APEX (Advance Purchase Excursion), which must be bought in advance and has certain other restrictions. The ITX fare for which air and hotel must be bought together is often the best fare on a major airline. There are other greatly discounted fares with and without advance-purchasing restrictions, offered only to or from certain destinations. Always call more than one airline and ask about all available types of fares. Packages with reduced fares may be obtained through airline tour desks or travel agents.

Flight Plans: A nonstop flight travels between two points without intermediate stops. A direct or through flight makes one or more stops en route, usually without a change of planes.

Wait List: You are unable to reserve a seat on a certain flight because it is completely sold out. Your name may be put on the wait list. If a cancellation comes up, you are notified.

Stand-by Fare: Travel fare when no reservations are made. Travel is subject to space availability at flight departure time. Fare may or may not be lower than the usual fare.

Transfer: Ground transportation by bus, van, limousine, taxi or other car between airports, resorts and hotels, or between two airports.

AIR CHARTERS

Advance Booking Charters (ABC): ABC offers a fixed price and date for a round trip or one-way charter flight. These are not regularly scheduled flights. Advance booking required.

Travel Group Charters (TGC): TGCs operate similarly to ABCs except that in an ABC the organizer takes a risk in meeting costs; on a TGC, the organizer earns a set fee. Therefore, vacant seats on the plane may increase the price for each passenger.

Affinity Pro-Rated Charters (APRC) are designed to serve the needs of organized groups whose members have a prior association.

THE FRUGAL TRAVELERS
$AVING $YSTEM

Before I get into the different kinds of travel options open to the Frugal Traveler, I would like to introduce the money-saving system central to this book and to truly enjoyable frugal travel experiences: the Frugal Travelers $aving $ystem. You should be keeping the ideas of this system in mind as we go through the information in the following chapters and as you begin to put together a frugal vacation.

The Frugal Travelers $aving $ystem (FT$$) is a systematic approach for all travelers to save money and to prevent and deal with problems related to travel. FT$$ is based on two words—A$k and A¢t. To the Frugal Traveler, A$k means *Always Seek Knowledge*. The reason the *S* in A$k is represented as a dollar sign is because the knowledge you are seeking, in relation to travel, has monetary value. According to your travel needs, the knowledge you seek is information about *real travel value*. Travel values and bargains are available to those who ask, who make the effort to find the information, and act on their findings. The A¢t portion of the Frugal Travelers Savings System stands for *The Aware and Cost-Conscious Traveler*. So, the "buy-words" of FT$$ are:

A$k—Always $eek Knowledge and A¢t—Aware and
Cost-Conscious Traveler.

A$k and A¢t are the keys to the Frugal Travelers method of saving money and dealing with travel problems. The cost of a trip, referred to in A¢t, should be considered in terms of the cost of your time, your comfort, your welfare and your money. It is only through the A$k process of the Frugal Travelers Saving System that the Frugal Traveler is able to find the real travel values on which he or she can A¢t.

For the Frugal Traveler, A$k is also an attitude and a philosophy of traveling for daily travel as well as for the larger travels through life.

With A$k and A¢t as your credo, you will first seek and then act on pertinent travel information. The Frugal Traveler minimizes the hassles and maximizes the rewards of traveling by using the Frugal Travelers $aving $ystem. By following this systematic approach to travel you will discover where to find the bargains, how to take advantage of them and what to do if a problem arises.

FRUGAL TRAVELERS
$AVING $YSTEM:

When it is time to A$k: Always seek knowledge—following that rule will get the best value for your money and avoid many travel problems. Then A¢t.

Since you must often ask others to get your best travel value, you should use these A$k guidelines:

- Be pleasant, and be friendly . . . but be reserved and cautious.
- Be persistent . . . but politely firm.
- Be knowledgeable . . . but never make the mistake of thinking you know it all.

When it is time to A¢t:

- Make check lists for planning your trip, for what you need to take and what you need to do before, and during, the trip.
- Buy and pay only for what you need and will actually use.
- Read the fine print.
- Use coupons and discounts as often as possible.
- Ask for supervisors and their superiors if not satisfied with responses and results.
- Know where you can go for help or better information.
- Keep your sense of humor and don't let problems spoil your fun—ignore minor irritations and annoyances, and relax and enjoy yourself!

Frugal travelers know how to do it all within their time and money budgets. Try the Frugal Travelers $aving $ystem—A$k and A¢t. It will work for you.

Since travel is so expensive, and you can waste or save hundreds to thousands of dollars with a single right-or-wrong decision, you should consider travel decisions a serious business. Many people save all year for a very special vacation. Anyone can save considerable amounts of money, even thousands of dollars, using Frugal Traveling techniques.

You may have already known of and done some of the things I talk about in this book. However, if you do not actually systematically do everything you can in the FT$$, then you may not really save as much money in the long run as you could and should. The idea is to do as much as you can. Do not put it off!

I hope that you are now on your way to becoming a Frugal Traveler, a traveler who makes wise decisions based on knowledge about all the available options, and who thus gets the best travel value for his or her dollars.

Once you become a Frugal Traveler you will be able to travel in style—a style you may once have thought was way above your means.

▪ 2 ▪

Yes! You Can Afford

Exotic Vacations –

An Enormous Variety of

Vacations are Available to

the Frugal Traveler

Package tours, charters, tie-ins, discount travel clubs—these can be confusing to even the most experienced traveler, yet it is often in these very offers that many of the best deals are found. The reason for this will become clear as we discuss each type of vacation, how to evaluate a particular deal, and where The Frugal Traveler can look to save money.

PACKAGE TOURS

For vacationers, package tours often offer a better deal than the traveler can get by booking each component of a trip separately. This is because tour operators buy large bulks of space on carriers and in hotels and thus get discounts usually unavailable to the individual traveler. It is not uncommon for a tour package— including a week's hotel stay at a minimum category hotel and airline tickets—to cost less than the price of the airline tickets alone. It really pays to check out tour packages available through ordinary travel agencies and through special discount agencies and clubs. You can save thousands of dollars doing this.

To know if the package price is best, check out the prices you could get on the components if bought separately. Some packages may come with extras you do not want or need. In off-peak seasons sometimes a "good package" becomes less of a good deal, as prices for hotel and car rentals and air or other transit may be reduced below package prices.

Check this tour package checklist to make sure you get the best deal you can:

- What is, and what isn't, included in the cost of the package?
- If tips are not included, how much money should you budget for tips? You may want to ask a travel agent for guidance on this because tipping customs vary greatly in different locales and situations.
- What types of accommodations are available?
- How much does it cost to upgrade, if you choose to do so, and do you have the option? Some packages are only worthwhile if upgrades in air seats or other transportation and lodging are available.
- How much time do you think you'll spend in your room? If you intend to use it a lot, you might want a larger or more elaborate room or the better view that comes with expensive accommodations.

- How much extra will you have to pay if you travel alone? Most lodging is based upon two people sharing a room. The average single room supplement can be from 10% to 70% above the per-person rate. There are sometimes discounts for a third or fourth person who shares the same room. If you are interested, ask!
- Many packages, especially if they include charter airfare, do not offer a discounted price to children. If you are traveling with children, this can make a package uneconomical. Choose a package that allows children who share their parent's room to stay free or at a sharply discounted rate.
- If your package includes airfare, but you do not live near the airlines or cruise pick-up point, see if the package you want offers free or reduced-rate air travel between your home city and the debarkation city.
- Find out if you can reduce the total cost of your package by making some arrangements that are usually part of the package yourself. If you live in or near the airline's hub city or your ship's port city, see if you can save money and time by taking the allowance and arranging your air travel separately. However, you'll usually save more money by taking the free airfare or the air add-on offered by the package.
- Know the name of each hotel you will be staying in and the exact type of accommodations you have paid for.
- Check if the following are included: tips, energy charges, departure taxes, baggage handling, airport and other ground transportation.
- Check which meals are included.
- Check which extras are covered, such as those for entertainment, city tours and entrance fees.
- Check the total number of nights you may stay in each city and in each hotel.
- Check the extent of the guided portion of your package, if any.
- Pay special attention to the *conditions clause,* usually found in the fine print.
- Check on the tour operator's past performance, amount of time in business, and reputation. Run your own check by

calling the U.S. Tour Operators Association, an industry regulatory group, at 212-944-5727. And, if possible, ask a travel agent's and previous tour participants' opinions.

READING THE FINE PRINT

Make sure to read *all* the fine print. It can save you many unpleasant surprises.

- Check how soon a deposit is required, and when the price-in-full is due. Decide how much in advance you want to commit yourself.
- Find out if the packagers retain the right to raise certain fees if their costs increase. Most large tour operators can and do absorb markups caused by currency fluctuations and minor cost increases from suppliers.
- Be sure the operator agrees to refund all your money if *he* cancels the trip.
- Check cancellation conditions and penalties. Don't put yourself in a position where you may have to forfeit some or all of your money. It is possible to buy trip-cancellation insurance from a travel agent, and you may want to check this out.
- Make sure you understand what is meant by the term "making substitutions" for items in a package. Don't get caught with a vacation different than the one you paid for.
- Check the overall value of a package. Compare the cost with what you would pay if you bought the components you really want and paid separately for each of them. Make careful comparisons of similar packages to determine real values.

You can afford a trip a little above your budget if you save by sharing accommodations, or take a less desirable room, or pass up optional luxuries. If you are traveling off peak or buying from a discount source, you may be able to get a trip usually above your budget. Shopping for the best package takes time and effort, but it's worth the reward in savings and the good trip you will have.

Some Other Things to Look for
When Considering a Package Plan

- Watch newspapers. Many resort areas advertise special rates for stays of a weekend or a week or more.
- When should you shop for a vacation tour? You should either buy early—to get the widest range of choices and early-bird specials—or you should wait until as late as possible to get last-minute and super-bargain discount deals.
- Be alert to possible hidden costs.
- During off-peak times all things may be cheaper, including transportation, lodging, food, etc. See if you can travel during these times.
- Check to make sure the hotel's location is conveniently close to where you're likely to be spending most of your time. If not, you're likely to pay more for transit than you thought.
- Are such basic amenities as a bathroom included? The fact that they might not be might surprise you, but you should check.
- Is the hotel of a good enough standard? You don't want to have to jump from the "base price" that attracted you to the package in the first place. If you prefer more comfortable or luxury accommodations, check on another package. On the same tour, two couples I know paid exactly the same price. One couple got a large room with a great view; the other couple got a small room that faced the back of a building. The tour operator's package called for run-of-the-house rooms—the hotel could assign a tour member to any available room. To be sure of a better room, buy a tour that specifically promises a certain class of rooms, such as "superior" or "ocean view" (see pp. 70-71).
- If you're paying on the installment plan, check annual interest rates. This can add up, so be aware.
- In foreign travel, paying in the foreign currency may or may not be to your benefit. Check this out.

IS YOUR BARGAIN REALLY A BARGAIN?

Everyone loves a bargain and it is a mistake not to take advantage of good ones. But be sure you understand that the conditions that make it a "bargain" may have big risks. Know the background of who you book a "bargain" through. There have been many travel industry bankruptcies. Make sure you use reliable travel clubs, operators and "bucket shops" (a travel agency that sells airline tickets at true discount prices). When you book through organizations that are not officially appointed or bonded agents of the carriers, the carrier is not responsible for your money.

A bargain is only a bargain if it makes sense for you. Be careful of misleading ads and very tight restrictions. Usually no refunds are available on these very much reduced bargain deals.

When reading travel advertisements and/or brochures, pay particular attention to the following:

- Small print or asterisks are sometimes used to alter the meaning of an advertising statement.
- Are current packages available at advertised prices?
- Words such as "extra charges," "discounted," "port taxes," "service charges" or "single supplement."
- If the brochure shows pictures of or talks about golf or tennis or other "frills," it can be misleading. It does not necessarily mean that these attractions will be included in the advertised price. Again, make sure you know exactly which features *are* included in the package price.
- Pay special attention to the contents of the "conditions" clause, usually found in fine print on the last page of the brochure: Is the price fixed, or "subject to" other things? What, again, are the cancellation penalties? What is considered a "valid reason" for either you or the tour operator to cancel the trip? What are the "major changes" under which a tour operator will give you a full refund? Some tour ads and brochures have misleading photos, showing items not included, but imply inclusion of "extras" or even unavailable features.

• Be alert for misleading prices in tour ads. Be cautious about buying what seems to be bargain tours. Do not assume that the figure quoted as a "regular price" is the regular retail price of the package tour—it could be the price of the tour components if purchased separately. It is even possible that by using the lowest available airfares you might be able to buy all the important components of a tour for less than the price of a package. And please note that "whenever possible," "of comparable value" or "package has the right to substitute" should be suspicious clauses to you.

A Quick Word on the Fully Escorted Tour: Escorted tours vary in the amount of time a guide will be with the traveler. Fully escorted tours are those in which travelers have a guide with them throughout the tour itinerary. However, there may be "free days," when travelers can be on their own.

Fully escorted tours are often best for a first trip to a foreign country. Many experienced travelers also prefer the cost efficiencies and convenience of a guided tour. During peak time, some very popular destinations are only available through guided tour packages, because large operators have bought out all existing space.

Families should know, however, that the escorted tour is probably the worst vacation for those traveling with small children. Children on most of these tours are treated as adults, and pay full adult prices.

THAT SPECIAL VACATION: THE CRUISE

Most people at some point dream of taking a cruise, and cruises are more affordable than most people think. There is a vast range of cruises available, and most travelers would enjoy this experience at some time in their life. The Frugal Traveler can get a terrific savings by booking a cruise at a discounted price during heavy price wars between competing cruise lines, or through a discount club or agency, and discounts are often available for last-minute bookings of cruise passengers.

Cruise packages can be a great value. You can vacation with

the rich and famous, who are traveling for regular prices, while you pay a low, discount price. Your total expenses can be pretty well ascertained in the planning stages, as cruises usually cover most of your expenses in the price of the cruise package—the cost of transportation, lodging, food, sports and recreational activities, entertainment and nightlife and airfare to and from the port of departure.

Among items usually *not* included in the quoted cruise price are: alcoholic drinks, port taxes, shore excursions, shopping and tips. Make sure, again, you understand what will and won't be part of the price of your cruise.

Cruises can vary in length from one day to several months, and itineraries vary from cruises down a river to cruises to exotic, far-off lands. Some boats carry just a few passengers, others carry thousands. There are also many special-interest cruises.

Since 40% of all cruise passengers are likely to be on their first cruise—less than 5% of adults in North America have ever taken a cruise—many people who are going to take a cruise will be inexperienced with this form of travel. For best value they might want to book through a travel agent or cruise specialist, using discounts wherever possible. Search for the cruise that best matches your interests, your lifestyle and your pocketbook.

In planning a cruise you should consider the following:

- Budget for trips. The Cruise Line International Association (CLIA) offers these helpful suggestions: the room steward and dining room waiter expect $2–$3 per person, per day; busboy and wine steward usually expect $1–1.50 per day. Tips are not offered to ships' officers or cruise directors, but bartenders and hairdressers are tipped as they are on land. For couples traveling on a 14-day voyage, tipping can add more than $200 to the cost of the cruise. Some cruise lines will let you charge tips to your credit card, so you might want to check into this.
- Find out what types of cabins are available and how much they cost. Although cabins are not segregated into different classes, a variety of accommodations in a wide range of prices does exist. Cabins that sell first are those at

the low and high ends of the scale. Size, amenities, location and sleeping arrangements improve as the cost increases.

- Find out how much extra it is to take a cabin without a roommate, if this situation applies to you. The surcharge varies, from 10 to 75%, and the average single supplement runs 50% above the per-person rate. Some lines will allow singles to travel alone in a cabin—at no extra cost—when they know a ship won't be fully booked. Ask.
- Many lines offer discounts if you share your cabin with three or more persons. Cabin space is often small, and more than two people may be uncomfortable. Ask, however, to see if there is a discount.
- Try to get free- or reduced-rate air travel between your home city and the ship's port. Air/sea deals are so common that about three-quarters of all cruise passengers now take advantage of them. Sometimes the air transportation is free.
- Another air/sea combination is the "add-on" type. Book a given cruise line and pay a small amount extra to fly to the port city from your hometown. Another type of add-on is the fly one way and cruise back in the other direction. Sometimes this is included in a package; other times there is an extra fee.
- Check if the price of a cruise reflects the cost of the "free" air travel. Many cruise lines offer a cruise-only allowance to passengers not needing the air portion. If you live in a large city and there is airfare competition, you may save money by taking the allowance. If you live in a smaller town, check if you can save money by taking the free airfare or the air add-on offered by the cruise line.

Important Tip: Cruise-arranged air transportation also makes it the cruise line's responsibility to ensure that you and your baggage make timely connections from the airport to the dock. This can be very important. If, for example, your plane is cancelled or delayed in your hometown, and you or your baggage do not catch the boat before it sails, and if you made your own connection arrangements—you could lose your whole payment for the cruise if you have no insurance. If, however, the cruise line makes the connection arrangements, they will have to accept the responsibility of getting you to the boat before it sails, arrange to pick you up somewhere else, or reimburse you for your costs.

A Few Specific Ideas for Cruise Bargains: If you want to take a transatlantic cruise, check out bargain fares on "positioning crossings," as for example, the sailing of a US- or Caribbean-based vessel from its home port to a European port, where it will be offering special summer cruises on its westward return sailing.

Sometimes you can cruise for up to 75% off. As the sailing time draws near you can get cabins that haven't been sold for enormous discounts.

For more information on anything having to do with cruising, write for a free copy of the Cruise Line International Association's booklet, *Answers to the Most Asked Questions About Cruising.* Send a self-addressed, stamped, business-size envelope to: Cruise Lines International Association, 17 Battery Place, Suite 631, New York, N.Y. 10004.

Club-Style Vacations: Club-style vacations, like Club Med and several others, are slightly different than either package tours or cruises. Everything is included in one single price per person. But even here, some give more than others: some include drinks and snacks, others don't; some allow no children; some allow no singles. Some regular hotels now successfully compete with clubs by including sports facilities and other extras in their prices. If you're going to use all or most of the facilities a club offers, they can be a great buy—otherwise the prices of many are high enough to make them unattractive to the Frugal Traveler.

You can evaluate any particular club offer; here's what's usually included:

- Round-trip air fare
- All transfers and baggage handling
- Accommodations (which may range from spartan to luxury)
- Local tours

- Breakfast, lunch, dinner daily, plus snacks
- Nursery and supervised camp facilities for children
- Unlimited drinks (not always: check)
- Crafts equipment and materials with instructors
- All sports and sports instruction, group or individual
- Nightly entertainment
- All hotel taxes, tips and gratuities

GREAT BARGAINS ARE AVAILABLE FROM DISCOUNT TRAVEL CLUBS

Discount travel clubs offer discounts on all sorts of travel, including further discounts on already bargain-priced packages. Also, some now offer a rebate of 5%–10% on any bookings that you find yourself that they book for you. Most of the services these clubs offer are beneficial only to the traveler who is flexible—as far as the destinations, hotels, duration, and day of trip departure. Most clubs arrange trips that are made up of wholesale travel suppliers' unsold inventory. Air only, as well as complete packages, are sold through these discounters.

Note: There are coupons for savings on membership fees to some of these discount clubs in the coupon section at the back of this book.

For the biggest discount prices on cruises and tours, your best bet is probably one of these last-minute travel clubs. They discount all kinds of tours, but you run the risk of not getting the trip you really want when you book through these clubs, and you must be flexible.

Specialist discount agencies, called "bucket shops," are probably best if your main goal is getting cheap airfare. Many specialize in certain destinations and can also get hotel discounts in those areas. Check your Sunday newspaper travel section for discount agency ads.

Note: Whenever you purchase a ticket from a bucket shop, read the fine print carefully—before you pay—to determine if any qualifiers or limitations are attached to the ticket's fare.

Bucket shops usually do not accept credit cards. Check them out with the local Better Business Bureau before you send them money. Some do not have great reputations.

THE BARGAIN TRAVELER'S CALENDAR

Knowing where and when to travel can save you up to 85% on a trip and enable you to enjoy surprising luxuries. Traveling off peak to fun and exotic locations is a sure way to get the most for Frugal Traveler dollars.

The carrier, hotel or other travel supplier decides what is peak and what is off peak, so that even in the same town one hotel can be on peak while others may be off peak. If you find out, by calling, which facilities have not yet raised their prices, you can travel during "peak" season for off-peak prices.

Smart travelers who can travel very close to the opening or closing dates of peak travel seasons—within a couple of weeks at either end of the season—may get the benefit of great weather, open attractions *and* the benefits of the much-reduced off-peak travel and lodging rates. In off-season one gets bargain prices and an opportunity to meet local people and to observe an area at its more natural pace. Visits during quieter times enable travelers to really get to know more about life in an area when the natives are not rushing around trying to make as much money as possible during the brief tourist season. Most major attractions are open, and many local cultural events take place during off-peak seasons that do not occur during high-peak seasons.

In some places, however, when the crowds are gone, the museums, stores, hotels, and other facilities may close and be unavailable to you. If there are specific things that you want to see, therefore, make sure they are open when you plan your visit, and try to go to places that benefit the off-peak visitors.

Check out the weather, including temperature and precipitation for the dates you plan to travel. Weather may be best during the bargain dates for many types of activities, such as sightseeing.

THE FRUGAL TRAVELER'S BARGAIN CALENDAR

UNITED STATES	*Expensive Travel Dates*	*Bargain Travel Dates*
Alaska	July, Aug.	Apr., May, & Sept., Oct.
Aspen, CO	Mid Dec.–Jan., Feb.–Mid Mar.	Apr.–Nov.
Cape Cod, MA	July, Aug.	Sept., June
Hawaii	Jan., Feb., Christmas	Oct., Nov.
Key West, FL	Mid Dec.–Late Apr.	May, June, July, Aug., Sept.
Las Vegas, NV	Oct.–Apr.	Mid May–June, July, Aug., Sept.
Miami, FL	Dec. 16–Apr. 30	May 1–Sept. 30
New Orleans, LA	Apr. 1–Aug. 31 Mardi Gras	Sept. 1–Mar. 31
New York, NY	Sept.–May 30	June, July & Aug.
Niagara, Falls, NY	June, July, Aug.	Sept.–May 30
Palm Springs, CA	Dec., Jan., Feb., Mar.	May–Sept.
Washington, DC	School holidays & June, July, Aug.	Jan., Feb., Mar.
Yosemite, CA	July, Aug.	May, June, Sept., Oct.
CANADA	July, Aug. Jan., Feb. in ski areas	May, June, Sept., Oct.
MEXICO		
Acapulco, Mex.	Mid Dec.–Mid Apr.	Mid Apr.–Mid Dec.
Cuernavaca, Mex.	Mid Dec.–Mid Apr.	Mid Apr.–Mid. Dec.
SOUTH AMERICA	Jan., Feb., Mar.	Apr., Dec.
EUROPE		
Austria	May–Sept. Dec.–Apr.	Oct., Nov.
Belgium	July, Aug.	May, June, Sept., Oct.
Czechoslovakia	Dec. 15–Mar. May, June, July, Aug.	Apr., Sept., Oct.

Yes! You Can Afford Exotic Vacations

Europe	Expensive Travel Dates	Bargain Travel Dates
Denmark	July, Aug.	May, June, Sept.
Finland	June 15–Aug. 15	May, June, Sept.
France	July, Aug. Easter–Sept. 30	June, Sept.
Great Britain	July, Aug.	Oct.–Mar.
Greece	Mid June–Mid Sept.	Early May–June, Late Sept., End of Oct.
Greek Islands	July, Aug.	May, June, Sept., Oct.
Holland	July, Aug.	Mid Apr.–June; Sept., Oct.
Hungary	June–Aug.	May, Sept.
Iceland	Mid June–Sept. 1	Sept. to May
Ireland	July, Aug., week of St. Patrick's Day	May, June
Italy	July, Aug., Dec., Feb. (ski resorts) Rome—Easter– Summer	Apr., May, June, Sept., Oct., Week of Jan 6, Special discounts for "white weeks" at ski resorts, Feb., Mar.
Luxembourg	Easter–mid Sept. June, July, Aug.	May, Late Sept.
Monte Carlo, Monaco	July, Aug.	May, June, Sept.
Norway	June, July, Aug., Christmas, Easter	May, Sept.
Poland	July, Aug., Festival	May, June, Sept., Oct.
Portugal	May–Oct.	Jan.–Apr. Nov., Dec.
Scotland	July, Aug.	May, June, Sept., Oct.
Spain	July, Aug.	Late June–Early Oct.
Sweden	End of June–Aug. 1	May, Aug., Sept.
Switzerland	Dec. 15–Apr. 15, Late May–Sept. 15	Late Apr., Late Sept.

Europe	*Expensive Travel Dates*	*Bargain Travel Dates*
West Germany	June–Aug.	Apr., May, Sept., Oct.
Yugoslavia	July, Aug.	May, Sept., Oct.
MIDDLE EAST		
Egypt	July, Aug.	Oct., Nov., Feb., Mar.
Elat, Israel	July, Aug.	Jan.–Mar., Nov.
Jerusalem, Israel	July, Aug., Christmas	Mar., Apr., May, Oct.–Dec.
Tel Aviv, Israel	July, Aug.	Feb.–June, Oct., Nov.
Turkey	May–Oct.	Nov.–Dec., Jan.–Apr.
FAR EAST		
Hong Kong, U.K.	July, Aug.	Apr., May, Sept., Oct., Nov.
Tokyo, Japan		May, June, Nov., Dec.
Peking, China	July, Aug.	May, June
India	July, Aug.	Apr., May, Sept., Oct., Nov.
PACIFIC OCEAN AREA		
Australia	October–March	June, July, Aug., Sept.
New Zealand	Nov.–Mar.	Mid Apr.–Nov.
Tahiti	Nov.–Mar.	Apr., May, June, July
CARIBBEAN AREA		
St. Thomas, Virgin Is.	Christmas–Mid Mar.	Apr.–Sept.
St. Croix, Virgin Is.	Christmas–Mid Mar.	Apr.–Sept.
Martinique I., Fr.	Christmas–Mid Mar.	Apr.–Sept.
Freeport, Grand Bahama	Dec. 1–Mar. 31	Apr. 1–Nov. 30
Bermuda	May, June, July, Aug.	Sept., Apr.
Holetown, Barbados	Jan., Feb.–Mid Mar.	Apr.–Sept.
Jamaica	Dec., Jan., Feb., Mar.,	Apr.–Sept.

Yes! You Can Afford Exotic Vacations

Caribbean Area	Expensive Travel Dates	Bargain Travel Dates
Nassau, Bahamas	Mid Dec.–Mid Apr.	Mid Apr.–Mid Dec.
Oranjestad, Aruba I.	Dec., Jan., Feb., Mar.	Apr.–Nov.
Philipsburg, St. Maarten	Christmas, Jan., Feb., Mar.	Apr.–Sept.
Pointe-à-Pitre Guadeloupe	Christmas, Jan., Feb., Mar.	April–Sept.
St. John's, Antigua	Dec., Jan., Feb., Mar.	Apr., May, June, July, Sept., Oct., Nov.
San Juan, Puerto Rico	Christmas, Jan., Feb., Mar.	Apr., Jan 1–10
Santo Domingo, Dom.Rep	Mid Dec., Jan., Feb., ar.	Apr., Early Dec.
Trinidad	Mid Dec., Jan., Feb.	Mar., Apr., May, Sept., Oct.

Flying

the Frugal Skies

Buying an airplane ticket today is easier than ever and yet the plethora of choices and options facing the Frugal Traveler can make the decision of exactly *what* to buy more difficult than it used to be. SuperSaver, MaxSaver, round-trip or one way—the inexperienced and even the experienced traveler is often at a loss as to which will save more money without creating undue inconvenience. This chapter is dedicated to shedding some light on this often-confusing, fast-changing subject.

WHAT WE'RE DEALING WITH

There is a wide range of airplane ticket prices available for almost all locations, and Frugal Travelers know that if they A$k and A¢t, they can pay thousands of dollars less for plane tickets than those sitting right next to them on the same plane.

Flying the Frugal Skies

When purchasing airplane tickets on regularly scheduled airlines or on some charter or small planes, there are certain ways to purchase your seats that can save you a lot of money— whether you are purchasing first class, business class, coach or economy category seats. To begin, first class is usually more than twice the price of economy class. Ask about this, because on some flights there is just a small amount to pay for an upgrade to first or business class. If you cannot purchase tickets in advance, or if you need to make several stopovers on the way to your final destination, or if you know in advance that you may have to cancel your flight or you cannot be restricted to a minimum or maximum stay, then first or business class may be a bargain for you. It could allow you the privileges you need for the least money and hassle. You may be able to buy first- or business-class tickets with all the privileges and travel comforts from a discount travel broker, coupon broker or other money-saving source. In fact, you may find you can pay the same for your tickets as others pay for very restrictive, advance payment, or nonrefundable coach or economy tickets. If you are told by an airline that a particular route is nonstop, some travel agents can arrange your booking on a one-way or round-trip ticket that allows you stopovers or routings that make your first or business class ticket a bargain. For example, you might be able to visit Spain and England on the way to France in business class, and not be limited in stop-over time. If you book a fare like APEX, however, you wouldn't be able to travel that same route without paying a lot more, since inter-country European flights are expensive when bought separately.

Business-class seats—less expensive than first class—are usually in the forward section of economy, often separated by a partition and, as in first class, liquor is usually free, headsets are free and there is a wider selection of menus, faster check-in facilities and roomier seats. You can buy one-way or round-trip tickets that have no minimum or maximum stay requirements, advance-purchase requirements or cancellation penalties, and you have the same unlimited stop-over privileges as first class.

Economy fares and requirements vary from airline to airline, and there may even be several types of economy fares available for a given trip on the same airline. Economy fares, as the name indicates, are much cheaper than first- and business-class tickets.

Excursion fares, which are for round-trips only, have minimum and maximum stays, and are usually much less expensive than even economy fares. Excursion fares vary greatly in their requirements and restrictions, both among airlines as well as within an airline, according to season and when and where you're traveling.

APEX, or Advance Purchase Excursion fares, are bargain fares that can save as much as 50% off economy fares for international travel. Note that these fares are usually less expensive than other excursion fares. APEX fares also apply to round-trips and have minimum and maximum stays.

Other special promotional fares available to the Frugal Traveler may be even less expensive, and may better meet special travel needs. For example, check out the possibility of taking advantage of GIT, or group-inclusive fares. This is often an excellent value for passengers traveling as a "group" on the same flight, and is usually obtained from a tour operator. These can be excellent travel buys, and you need not know or ever get involved with the others in your group. Investigate all details, costs and restrictions. Sometimes, even if the land arrangements are not what you want, it is cheaper to take one of these tours and simply not use the land arrangements, since the airfare can be such a good buy. Sometimes the come-on price for air *and* hotel is cheaper than the price of the cheapest available airfare! But make sure that restrictions are not too severe.

Also, check out smaller airlines that compete with major carriers by offering cheaper fares, roomier seats, and/or extra frills, and have less restrictions for the same travel route.

An Important Note About the Benefits of Travel on Major Carriers: If there is a cancellation of your flight, another major carrier may have other flights to place you on to get you to your destination. There are reciprocal agreements among most major carriers that allow you to travel on another airline if your flight is cancelled—at no additional charge to you, regardless of the class of seat available on the reciprocating carrier. Smaller airlines usually do not have these reciprocal arrangements; all they can do is refund your money.

Call all airlines servicing the areas you will visit. When you

think you have the deal you want, make your booking immediately. Be sure you know and understand the specifications,
including those for departures and connections, cancellation
penalties and requirements, stay requirements and other details.
Always check the travel pages of your local newspaper for the
latest announcements of special promotional fares. Pay attention
to price wars and to announcements of unusual fare reductions.
Listen for announcements of mergers or buy-outs of airlines and
for air routes or new routes being added to an airline—this is
often a signal that discounted fares may soon become available.

MORE TIPS: FINDING THE BEST FARE

- Two-thirds of all airline tickets are now sold by travel
  agents, so they are a good source of information on discounts. And you should be aware of the fact that nearly
  90% of all US air travelers flew on discount fares last year.
- Most major domestic airlines now have two types of discount fares, offering savings of up to 50% off standard
  coach fares. One of these, the SuperSaver, is a round-trip
  fare. An airline will sell only a certain number of seats at
  this price. In most markets, there are different types of
  SuperSavers, and savings vary depending upon the advance-purchase requirement, length of stay and days of
  travel (midweek or other times).
- In many markets, the major domestic carriers also offer a
  capacity-controlled but unrestricted coach fare, priced
  20–25% below regular coach. There are many other discounts offered by established airlines as well as by the
  large and small commuter airlines, which have thousands
  of different joint fares combined with discounts as Super-
  Savers.
- You will find that international airfares are more uniform
  than US airfares. This is because a pricing cartel sets fare
  levels for most international airlines. The international
  round-trip discount airfare used most is the APEX fare,
  which can save passengers at least 50% of the standard
  coach rate. Restrictions vary from country to country.
- Be sure you understand the restrictions on a discount fare.

Most airline discounts require advance purchase. If you change your itinerary after the advance-purchase deadline, the carrier will recompute your ticket price, and this can sometimes more than double your cost.

If you wait to pay your airfare after you've made a telephone reservation, and the airline raises the fare overnight, you'll pay the higher fare.

- Changing planes on domestic flights can be less expensive than flying nonstop, but not necessarily. Be warned that sometimes it costs more.

- Compare prices for leaving from different airports in the same general area. This can save you as much as 60% of your fare. The bigger airports have more discounts available than the smaller airports, although sometimes at a secondary airport some airlines may offer specials to increase their business there. To take advantage of these lower rates, it might be worthwhile to get a ride to the airport where you can get the best price.

- Airlines sell most of the cheapest tickets during off-peak flights, even during peak season, and during off-peak hours or off-peak days of the week. If you have a flexible schedule, consider this an opportunity to save.

CHARTER FLIGHTS AND PACKAGES

Charter packages can offer terrific deals, because their operators buy large blocks of space on a flight or may even commission an entire plane. These bargain airfares are most frequently sold with hotel arrangements and ground transportation—sightseeing and meals are also frequently sold as required or optional parts of the package. The prices of these packages are often less than economy or excursion fares alone, if you or your agent were to book them independently. The different packages and the actual savings for each vary tremendously. There are luxury packages that include the most up-scale properties and adventures, and there are packages for lower-budget travel itineraries. The price you pay may depend on how many days you intend to stay, what day of the week you leave and the time of year.

Make sure you read the fine print of your charter contract before you sign it. A charter may use a regular airline or a special, charter-only airline. Remember when you book a charter that, even if you fly on a regularly scheduled airline, your contract is with the tour operator or agent, not the airline. If the tour operator goes out of business, you could lose your money.

On most charters, if you change your plans you incur a large financial loss. If you cancel several weeks in advance, some charters will only charge you a cancellation fee, but on other charters you can lose all your money if you decide to cancel and do not have cancellation insurance. Check and see if the charter has the right to cancel, or if they have the right to make drastic changes in your arrangements like changes in price, itinerary and hotel. You may not want the trip with these changes, and you may or may not have the right to cancel under the new circumstances. If you decide to cancel due to the changes, you may find making other arrangements difficult on such short notice—especially if this occurs during peak season.

Here are important travel-industry secrets: Although policies regarding tickets are strict, they can be circumvented. Passengers holding discounted tickets, which are supposedly nonrefundable, as customers with a doctor's note attesting they were sick, can usually get a refund if they miss their flight. Many major airlines allow holders of nonrefundable tickets who miss their flight but still make it to the airport within two hours of their departure, to fly standby on the next available flight. Also, carriers waive the rule of nonrefundability and issue refunds if bad weather closes an airport or if a flight is canceled because of mechanical problems. Although it is not always publicly admitted, frequent flyers club members find it easier to get restrictions overlooked and are able to make many ticket changes and discounts despite ticketing rules.

Also, some big travel agencies can get airlines to overlook advance-purchase requirements and honor tickets bought when a passenger cannot meet purchase or flight schedule requirements.

Some Other Ways to Stretch Your Travel Dollar: In addition to saving money on the general booking of a flight, those who wish to purchase luxury for less money find there are several options:

- Some airlines with two-class service offer business or first class at fares well below major airline business- and first-class fares. These high-quality options are more expensive than coach/economy on smaller airlines and on competitive airlines, but the added comfort and services are often well worth the small extra cost.
- You can enjoy high-quality service at affordable prices with a frequent flier coupon for first-class travel. You can purchase them from frequent fliers who can't use them. From $1500 to $2400 you can buy a coupon good for first-class travel to Europe or the Pacific—travel that would cost up to $7000 at regular, major airline prices. Comparable values are available for domestic travel and travel to other areas abroad.

Investigate Discount Travel Clubs, Brokers, Clearinghouses: Discount travel clubs and other organizations like them can provide incredible savings on airfare and other travel arrangements. They have telephone hotlines that are updated daily with new trip choices, and I've constructed a list here of some of the better-known companies the Frugal Traveler might want to contact. This is not an endorsement of any of these organizations.

Airhitch/Worldwide Destinations Unlimited, 2901 Broadway, Suite 100, New York, NY 10025, 212-864-2000. Registration fee required. Cut-rate vouchers for airfare to Europe. You cannot pick exact date or exact destination of flight, but the fare is very cheap.

Access, 250 West Fifty-seventh Street, Room 511, New York, NY 10019, 212-333-7280. Membership fee required. Select exact date and destination.

Discount Travel International, 7563 Haverford Avenue, Philadelphia, PA 19151, 215-668-2182. Membership fee required.

Encore Short Notice, 4501 Forbes Boulevard, Lanham, MD 20706, 301-459-8082. Membership fee required.

Last Minute Travel Club, 6A Glenville Avenue, Allston, MA 02134, 617-267-9800. Membership fee required.

Moments Notice, 40 East Forty-ninth Street, New York, NY 10017, 212-486-0503. Membership fee required.

On Call to Travel, 11739 SW Beaverton Highway, Suite 120, Beaverton, OR 97005, 503-643-7212. Membership fee required.

Stand Buy Limited, 311 West Superior Street, Chicago, IL 60610, 312-943-5737. Membership fee required.

Vacations to Go, 5910/D Westheimer, Houston, TX 77057, 713-974-2121. Membership fee required.

Worldwide Discount Travel Club, 1647 Meridian Avenue, Miami Beach, FL 33139, 305-534-2082. Membership fee required.

You can get discount tickets and packages from these clubs for prices that are at least 20–60% below the airlines' lowest promotional fares.

GETTING BUMPED, LOSING YOUR BAGGAGE, AND OTHER TRAVEL TRIBULATIONS

Every traveler has either experienced or heard of some of the problems or emergencies associated with air travel. Once the Frugal Traveler has booked a flight, he or she can also benefit from knowing how to deal with something unexpected, should it occur. Frugal Travelers know how to make many emergencies work for them rather than against them.

Getting Bumped: How to Make It Pay: Getting "bumped" is when you are asked to leave an oversold flight. Airlines overselling seats is a common practice which results in their sometimes having to take passengers off a flight that is oversold. They oversell because they have so many no-shows on so many of their flights, especially during holidays, when the no-show rate can surpass 25%. In December nearly twice as many air travelers are bumped as during the slower months. There are risks and rewards you should know about if you volunteer or are "bumped" from a flight on which you have a seat. Law requires the carrier to seek volunteers who will give their seats in exchange for some type of compensation.

To qualify for denied boarding compensation if you get bumped, you must hold a confirmed reservation and you must have bought your ticket before the deadline set by the airliner, usually at least 30 minutes prior to departure time. You must also have met the airline's check-in requirements: the usual domestic check-in deadline is 30 minutes before departure, but on international flights check-in time may be as much as one or two hours before departure.

The amount of compensation offered depends upon the length of the delay incurred and how badly the airline needs your seat. The airline doesn't have to pay you if it can book you on a flight that arrives within one hour of your originally scheduled arrival time, but it will if they want your seat. They will put you on the next available flight, and you use your original ticket on the new flight. If you arrive more than one hour but less than two hours later than originally scheduled (up to four hours later on international flights), the carrier must by law pay you the cost of your ticket or $200, whichever is less. And if you arrive more than two hours late (more than four hours late on international flights), the airline must pay you double the cost of your ticket, or $400, whichever is less.

Instead of cash, however, the airline may offer you a free ticket on a future flight, as long as the flight's cost is equal to or greater than that of the flight from which you were bumped. You may decline the offer and insist upon the money. Most US airlines now offer a free round-trip ticket to any of their domestic destinations, to be used within a year.

An advanced boarding pass and seat assignment may imply that you are guaranteed a seat, but in fact it guarantees you nothing until you actually check in. Therefore, if you don't want to get bumped, check in at the gate as early as possible.

Tip: Sometimes, when you make a reservation, the clerk will try to indicate on your record an earlier check-in time than is required. After that time, your record could be wiped from the computer. Always insist that the latest time required is entered on your computer record, since you never know when you might be unavoidably delayed—and try to call if you know you will be arriving late.

Making Money Playing the Bumping Game:
Raise your hand too soon and you may get less compensation than you would get if you waited for a better offer. Don't wait *too* long

or you could lose your chance to be bumped and perhaps fly free.

If you're flying on a route with frequent air service and you arrive at the gate to find your flight has oversold, volunteer to forfeit your seat. If there are no volunteers and you haven't volunteered to give up your seat, you won't be eligible for compensation since the airline will probably be able to book you on a flight arriving within an hour of your original flight. If you volunteer you might obtain some compensation for the hour's delay.

If you think your flight is oversold and you are willing to give up your seat in return for compensation, pay close attention to the announcements made just prior to departure. If you are already on the plane, sit as close to the front as possible. This increases your chances of being chosen if the airline has many volunteers.

If your flight is delayed, passengers are offered at least one free long-distance telephone call, meals at the airport if delay is past meal time and lodging if the delay is overnight and you are not in your home city.

If a flight is cancelled for mechanical reasons the airline does not have to pay compensation for your missing out on a prepaid vacation, even if you miss your cruise boat or tour.

Baggage: If a bag is delayed the airline is not required to deliver it to a passenger, although most will. If you ask, some airlines will offer a traveler a kit with essential toiletries, and some will offer cash to pay for essentials. They will probably not pay for the full cost of new clothing. Negotiate with the airline.

Travel light. This is one of the most important points for a successful trip. Plan an all-purpose, multi-use, mix-and-match wardrobe, appropriate for the situations and climate and coordinated with one or two basic solid colors. It is cheaper than buying a lot of accessories and outfits that do not mix and match.

If you cannot manage your own baggage, you are taking too much. Often travelers find themselves without porters and have to carry everything so be prepared for this.

FLY IN STYLE,
EVEN AT BARGAIN PRICES

If you are flying coach, you can have a large choice of good meals that are much better than regular coach meals if you call and order the meal of your choice from a menu at least 24 hours before flying.

- For more room, fly certain airlines, especially smaller ones that often provide roomier seats in coach, or reserve seats near bulkheads and exit doors.
- If you want more room for sleeping or just stretching out, ask the reservations attendant whether it is a full or lightly booked flight and, if it seems to have space, see if you can get seated where there are seats on either side of you that will be empty.
- For prompter cocktail and food service, book the lower numbered seats on most planes—up front you also stand a better chance of getting your beverage and meal of choice before they run out.

• 4 •

Follow Frugal Paths:

On the Road

Renting a car is generally an easy thing to do but, as anyone who has done so recently can tell you, the variety of options and different rates available today make the decision of what's a bargain and what's not more difficult than it used to be. The Frugal Traveler, therefore, needs to know how car rental companies operate—both here and abroad—so he or she can effectively do business with them and navigate a course to the best possible deal. This chapter is dedicated to helping you find the best wheels for the best price so that, once you find yourself where you want to be, you can, if you wish, move around quickly and easily and trouble-free.

SOME CAR RENTAL COMPANIES

The following companies are multinationals, with rental operations in both the US and Europe: Ansa (American International in the US), Avis, Budget, Europcar (National in the US), Hertz, and InterRent (Dollar in the US). Six others—Auto Europe, Connex, Cortell, Europe by Car, Foremost, and Kemwel—are wholesale tour operators based in the US. They arrange for cars through suppliers in Europe (often including the multinationals). The multinationals usually offer greater flexibility in reservations and payment options, but wholesalers often have better prices.

No one company offers the best car rental deal for every car or in every location. Within a single country, one company may offer the lowest price on the one car that is the advertised special, and at the same time be overpriced on other cars. You have to check competitors to locate the best buy in any area.

If you are going to rent a car, plan for it before your trip. You will have a better chance at getting the car you want at the price you want. You may not get the car you want, especially during peak season, without advance planning and reservations.

After you reach your destination, you may discover a local car-rental agency that offers a better deal for your itinerary. You can keep the car you originally rented for a minimum time and then rent another car for the duration of your trip.

These are the most important things to keep in mind as you go about renting a car:

- The advertised price is almost always per person, and requires a minimum of two people. Double the advertised price when you are comparison shopping (single travelers pay a supplement).
- Bargain rental rates usually require making arrangements in advance—even before you leave the US—if you are going abroad.
- Payment can be in advance or upon your return of the car and you can pay by cash or by credit card.
- Wholesalers require advance reservations and full prepay-

ment one to six weeks in advance. If they handle reservations with a shorter lead time, you'll have to pay the extra cost of long-distance calls and the express delivery of vouchers.

• The cost of insurance adds greatly to the daily rental costs. Figure these in, too, when deciding if you want to rent a car. The costlier the car you rent, the higher the cost of insurance will be.

• Do not underestimate the importance of renting a car from an agency with many offices and drop-off points along your itinerary. Car problems requiring turning in one car and picking up another are a real headache if you are not within easy driving distance of a company outlet.

EUROPE ON WHEELS: RENTING A CAR OR RIDING THE RAILS

Since traveling in Europe is such an important part of the plans of so many of us at some time, it is wise to consider Europe in particular, bearing in mind that these are generalities that hold true for any travel.

Whether to travel by rail or car depends on many things. The choice between driving and taking the train is a question of travel preference, cost, road and other conditions in the country in which you are traveling. It cannot be said that one is always cheaper than the other—it all depends on what you plan to do, how much traveling you intend to do, how long you will need a car, where you will be going and the number of people in your party.

Renting a Car: What the Frugal Traveler Should Know

• If you plan to drive, you should first settle on the kind and size of car you *need*. For international or interstate travel, decide if a single-country (state) rental will suit your purposes, or if you need a one-way car (pick up in one country or state, return in another).

• If you're going to be driving for a month or more you should consider arranging your itinerary so that you can conveniently *lease* a car.

• If you decide to rent a car it's smartest to investigate prices and make a reservation before you leave home. This way you won't be stranded, especially if you're traveling during a busy time or in a busy area. If, however, you decide to rent a car after you've arrived in Europe, you can often save money—when a reservation must be made from the states—by making a transatlantic call to the US office of a multinational that offers special touring promotional rates with short advance reservation.

- It is usually most economical to rent a car with unlimited mileage for one week at the base rate plus taxes, with adjustment for exchange rate (if any).
- Remember to figure in the applicable taxes which are added on to your bill but not quoted in the prices—up to an astronomical 33.3% in some countries, like France. You can save money if you rent a car and start your trip in a country that charges less taxes, if other costs are similar and you plan to visit the country with the cheaper taxes during your trip.
- The cost of renting a car for additional weeks may not be the same as for the first week.

Tip: Extras vary in cost, sometimes depending on the area. In Europe it's hard to find inexpensive rental cars with air-conditioning, whereas in Israel all but the least expensive cars usually include air-conditioning.

One-Way Rentals: With many companies you're allowed to rent a car in one city and return it in another, within the same country. Only a few highly restricted programs require you to return the car to the office where you rented it.

If you want to return the car in a different country, however, you do have some options. A few rental firms allow cars rented in one country to be returned in another country at no extra cost—check their brochures for details. Costs and taxes in those cases are determined by the rates in the country where you pick up and rent the car. This can be your best alternative if your itinerary can conform to the company's free-return policy.

Road & Rail Combinations: Look for car rental companies that offer "Drive One Way" plans. Under these plans cars can be picked up and returned at any combination of many major cities. The base rate is usually higher than most single-country rates. You usually don't have to pay any tax on a one-way rental that originates in countries in Europe, for example, other than Denmark, France, or Sweden. Ask about the tax on all one-way rentals. Car-rental packages change constantly, with increases and decreases in prices according to season, competition, promotional discounts and rules and regulations.

- Some car-rental companies have good discounts for car rentals tied in with foreign rail service, for those seeking value yet do not want to drive too much.
- Car rental costs vary substantially by country, even for identical cars. Currently, the European countries with the lowest rental rates are, in order of increasing cost, Spain, Luxembourg, Portugal, Germany and the Netherlands.
- The cost of renting a car abroad varies in value depending on if the dollar is up or down.
- The tax on rental cars also fluctuates—in Portugal it has increased from 8% to 16% while in Spain the tax has dropped from 33% to 12%.
- Consider starting a road trip in the country or state that has the lowest rental-car rates. In Europe, start in Portugal or Spain rather than in a more expensive country such as Switzerland or France. Be aware that countries with high rates often have small taxes or VATS (Value Added Taxes), and vice versa. (One way around the VAT is to rent your car in one country where there is little or no VAT and drop it off in another.)
- Some large firms have plans that allow no-cost pickup and drop-off in certain cities. However, such charges can be substantial, and the weekly rental rates for such plans are much higher and payment must be made and cities specified in advance. Rates and plans vary widely, so ask!
- If you're staying in Europe for a month or less it is usually cheapest to rent a car, but if you'll be there for one to three months, check out leases. For a longer stay, buy the car and bring it home with you. The French especially encourage leasing, since their laws allow tourists to lease a

new car without paying the VAT, which saves lessees a heavy 33% of the original cost.

- Brochures for car rentals in foreign countries often quote rates in dollars. This may not be more than a guide, though, because currency rate fluctuations determine what you pay at the time you make your booking—not the rates when the brochure was written.
- Always look for free-mileage plans if you plan to drive long distances. Most of the big rental car companies allow some free mileage. Smaller companies usually offer more free miles and charge less cents per additional mile or even offer unlimited free miles. The policy varies with location. In tourist areas unlimited mileage packages from all size companies are not uncommon.

Tip: Don't consider taking a rental car out of Britain. The insurance costs are prohibitive. Rent a separate car after you travel across the English Channel. Also, don't bring a rental car into Mexico.

Tip: Be aware of age requirements for both renting and driving a car. Usually the minimum age is 21 and the maximum age is 70. However, 30 is the minimum age in some places. Investigate before you pay.

In the US: Those traveling by car in the US, especially those planning to use their own car, should consider joining an auto club. Joining an auto club can help you save money, and many auto clubs have travel benefits in addition to their regular helpful services—including discounts on car rental, lodging and group travel benefits. Investigate before you join, as club benefits vary widely.

If you have a bank credit card, check to see if they have an affiliated auto club, and if they offer car rental and lodging discounts.

What follows is a list of some of the bigger auto clubs in the US. Call or write them if you want further information. (This is not an endorsement of any of these clubs.)

Allstate Motor Club, 34 Allstate Plaza,
Northbrook, IL 60062, 312-291-5461, 800-323-6282

American Automobile Association (AAA), 8111 Gatehouse
Road, Falls Church, VA 22047, 703-222-6000

Amoco Motor Club, Box 9048, Des Moines, IA 50369,
800-334-3300

Chevron Travel Club, Box P, Concord, CA 94524,
415-827-6000

Exxon Travel Club, Box 3633, Houston, TX 77253,
713-680-5723

Montgomery Ward Auto Club, 200 North Martingale Rd.,
Schaumburg, IL 60194, 800-621-5151.

National Automobile Club, 3800 Wilshire Boulevard,
Los Angeles, CA 90010, 213-386-6591

Shell Motorist Club Plus, Box 2463, One Shell Plaza,
Houston, TX 77001, 713-241-6161

Texaco Star Club, Box 224669, Dallas, TX 75222,
214-258-2060

United States Auto Club, Box 660460, Dallas, TX 75266,
800-348-2761

Suggestions for the Motorist: It's most economical to make sure that everything is in good repair before your trip. You'll use less fuel and get better efficiency from your car, and avoid costly emergency repairs. Join an auto club to help you plan your trip, and to help you with information, insurance coverage, and emergency and repair service along the way. The National Institute for Automotive Service Excellence publishes a directory of about 10,000 repair shops all over the U.S. which employ certified mechanics. It is available from NIASE, Suite 515, 1825 K Street N.W., Washington, DC 20006. Also, see the valuable coupons for products and services in the back of this book.

RIDING THE RAILS:
A DIFFERENT WAY TO GET AROUND

This can be a wonderful, romantic, adventurous way to travel—on good rail systems, as in many parts of Europe—or it can be a horror when the system is bad.

On many trains, you must have advance reservations to get a seat. Many discount fares are only valid with certain advance purchases, and many only if you purchase them before you leave the US or some other specific country. Others are available only through specific organizations, clubs and tourist offices. Some bargain fares can only be purchased in the country in which traveling will be done, while still others are never available in the country concerned.

As always, you must plan your trip to get the best buys in train travel. In many countries the fare is based on the distance traveled and the class of accommodations. If your plans include a lot of train travel, a rail pass is usually a good bargain, and many can be purchased at discount prices. In addition, having a rail pass ahead of time saves hours of standing in line for tickets at busy ticket offices every time you want to travel.

Costs for rail travel change constantly. The cost of a Eurailpass, BritRail Pass and most other country and regional rail passes goes up every year. Frugal Travelers can defray some of the rising costs by constantly checking for the best current promotional discounts.

The following are some of the things the Frugal Traveler should keep in mind when considering travel by rail.

• Keep in mind that train travel is especially convenient if you concentrate mainly on cities. The train usually takes you right downtown, and you obviously don't have to worry about parking. On the other hand, if you'd like to explore rural areas, a car is often best for flexibility and convenience.

- Although a rental car may provide greater flexibility, a rail pass reduces the confusion of navigating in a foreign country.

The Rail Pass: There are so many choices that selecting a rail pass can be quite complicated. Rail pass information is best obtained from railway offices or government tourist offices or from a good travel agent. You should be aware of the fact that prices are subject to change without notice.

Tip: Walking, obviously, is a great money saver. Many cities are laid out so you can easily walk to visit important sites and shopping areas and other monuments.

Tip: If you are staying close to the center of town, you will save on transportation. It's worth a little extra money to stay where you don't have a big trip every day to get to the areas where you'll be spending your time.

CABS, BUSES AND BOATS

Before we leave this chapter on car, train and ground transportation in general, I should say a few words about some of the other methods of getting around while traveling.

Cabs are expensive in many cities. Cab rides from the airport to your hotel or those taken to go shopping may cost a fortune. Check it out before you go. Take the bus or train wherever possible if you want to economize.

You can save money by knowing some of the "dangers" lurking in using cabs. Late at night, taxis at airports, train and bus stations sometimes refuse to use their meters and demand a flat rate, sometimes 50% or more higher than normal. Taxis at airports often overcharge tourists for their luggage and drivers can adjust their meters so that it counts twice the speed.

The driver can take you on a longer route to the hotel and charge you more, or the driver may tell you about a great restaurant or hotel just because he gets a cut if he gets you to go there. These warnings apply to only a small number of cabbies. There *are* many wonderful cab drivers, filled with good-natured advice and news, so tip accordingly. Try to determine from a local person what the approximate fare will be before entering a taxi so that you'll have some basis for judgment.

Bus situations vary. Check out bus routes and service in individual countries and cities. There are many discounts available. Many bus lines have discount tie-ins with rail or boat transportation. Many bus routes are international or interstate. Contact tourist bureaus.

For those wishing to travel by boat, many companies offer 20%–25% off for seniors or those with student identification cards, and many have tie-ins with other passes, like rail or bus discount passes. For more information, contact tourist bureaus.

• 5 •

Living in Luxury

On Your Budget

One of the most enjoyable things about vacations, and about travel in general, is the feeling of being away from the usual routine and of staying in some place other than home. Many people dream of staying just one night at the Ritz, to even briefly feel what it's like to be catered to in grand style. Many consider a weekend at almost any place other than home a sort of vacation.

Indeed, many people consider plane and train and bus and car travel merely a means to an end, different ways to get to where they want to be. In previous chapters we've looked at certain frugal ways of flying to a chosen destination, and traveling about once one gets there. Now it's time to take an equally frugal look at accommodations.

This chapter is dedicated to helping the Frugal Traveler find and secure the accommodations of his or her desires and even, perhaps, his or her dreams.

TO BEGIN

A "frugal" vacation can be spent in a good value, posh resort, or in a budget motel or charming country inn. A budget vacation means careful spending at all times, and careful budgeting before and during your trip. But even on a limited budget, plan to splurge occasionally to keep the trip fun.

If you are on a budget, pick less expensive places to visit. For example, big cities are costlier than rural areas so you can stay at better class accommodations in areas where costs in general are less. In some areas there is not too much difference in price between budget- and premium-level lodging facilities. This is true both domestically and outside the US.

Thus, if you stay in a charming hotel, or inn, or bed-and-breakfast guest house, surrounded by people anxious to serve you amidst wonderful antiques, you'll feel like a millionaire on any budget.

If you're undecided on where to go, go to where it is most economical. There is a big difference in living costs once you are at your destination. Recently a dinner I had in a city cost $80 per person. For a comparable dinner in Mexico, I spent $10 per person. Quite a difference!

WHAT THE FRUGAL TRAVELER SHOULD KEEP IN MIND WHEN ARRANGING LODGING

During off-peak travel, when an area gets the least travelers, inexpensive rates are available. It is also possible for independent travelers to find more of their own bargains during off peak. Keep in mind what is off-season in most places may become peak season for other special interest areas.

In many places there are tremendous variations in seasonal rates. Here's a seasonal rate sample from the top hotels on a

Caribbean Island. Deluxe category rooms went from $225 in winter high season to $155 in spring and fall mid season. In summer or low season, a standard room costs $85 and a deluxe room $100. Hotels may give lower rates for stays of three nights or more, especially off peak—and during this time you usually do not have to take meals—so you save on food and service tax if you want to eat at less expensive restaurants.

Many large in-city hotels encourage weekend guests by offering special rates. When you take advantage of special deals, you can afford some of the hotels you thought were way beyond your means. You'd be surprised.

Make sure that parking is included in your package, even in big city hotels. Parking in urban areas can be very expensive. Also find out in advance if the hotel at which you are planning to stay is on the regular route of an airport bus or group limousine service so you can cut ground transfer costs.

You can save money when traveling through larger cities by making reservations, whenever possible, in cities on the weekends and at resorts on the weekdays. Although credit cards are not always honored in low-cost establishments, they can still be invaluable in an emergency. Look into lodgings where a travel-management company offers negotiated rates even lower than corporate rates.

Again, save by avoiding the crowded spots. Don't go at the height of the season to the popular national parks, or visit a jammed resort. Instead, select one of the less-crowded areas that is just as good or better.

Adjust your travel style to the circumstances. Some hotel chains have a wide variety of category accommodations all within the same chain, from luxury to budget, so you can still use that hotel when you want to economize. Pay only as little or as much as necessary to get the standard of lodging you *really* want.

Hotel discounts are an important part of the services offered by travel clubs and other specialty organizations. See the coupon section at the back of this book.

If you are looking for hotel value one of the best ways to find it is by looking at brochures. A brochure can call a hotel first class, but when you get there you find that the hotel does not meet your expectations. According to the classification system of that particular country, however, that hotel may very well be first class. Without a recommendation from someone you will probably select a hotel based on a hotel classification system, and these systems can be seriously misleading. You assume that in hotel grading, as in the airline class system, first class represents the best available when actually first class represents something closer to the midpoint than the top of the quality scale.

Many governments—national, provincial, state and local— have official hotel classifications. Most use four to six major gradations, indicated by numbers of stars or classes. Belgium has four ratings, the lowest being one star and the highest being four stars. Spain has five ratings, the lowest one star and the highest five stars, so if you didn't know the actual classification system for that country, you might think that Belgium's four-star hotel is not as good as Spain's five-star hotel, while actually both ratings are for the top hotels in the country. Some governments use letter classifications such as A through F. Government classification systems are usually the most comprehensive and detailed of all classification systems.

HOTEL RATING GUIDE

Each guidebook also has its own rating system. Several hotel reference books of this type are published for use by travel agents, and one of the most widely used is the *Official Hotel and Resort Guide* (OHRG), which classifies according to nine categories:

- Superior Deluxe: An exclusive and expensive luxury hotel offering the highest standards. The world's top hotels are in this category.
- Deluxe: An outstanding hotel offering many of the same features as Superior Deluxe. These hotels may offer more reasonable rates than Superior Deluxe hotels.
- Moderate Deluxe: A Deluxe hotel, but with less qualifications. Some accommodations or public areas may not be up to Deluxe standards.
- Superior First Class: An above-average hotel.

- First Class: An average, comfortable hotel.
- Moderate First Class: A First Class hotel slightly below average.
- Superior Tourist Class: A budget hotel usually with well-kept, functional accommodations.
- Tourist Class: Strictly budget lodging, with some facilities or features of Superior Tourist Class. In developing nations, these can be a horror for American tourists.
- Moderate Tourist Class: Very low-budget, often old and not well-kept.

Ask which classification system your travel brochure, travel agent or lodging establishment is using. If it is based on five stars, and four stars is the largest number listed in your tour package, you're not in the best room in the hotel. Ask!

Recommendations for hotels in some guidebooks and by some travel agents concentrate on high-priced, "safe," well-known names. Travelers looking for inexpensive lodging should consult budget-travel guides and ratings in current official government publications. If a travel agent makes a hotel recommendation, ask if the recommendation is based on firsthand knowledge; if it is not, consult an up-to-date guidebook.

GO AFTER THE PRICE YOU WANT

First decide exactly what you want, what you want to spend, and where you want to go. Do you want a full-service hotel, a budget motel, a charming guest house? Frequently, hotel, transportation, and product rates are open to negotiation. Finding a good deal on a room or a taxi or other transportation is often simply a matter of asking for one. Don't underestimate the power of bargaining. You may bargain and stay where you thought was beyond your budget.

Here are some bargaining tactics for getting lodging bargains:

- At small hotels, if you are reserving a room for a lengthy stay, offer to pay in advance for a discount in return.
- Look for a hotel with few cars in the parking lot. Arrive after 6:00 PM. The later you check in, the better your

chances of getting a bargain. (If you really need a room, however, arrive at the reservation desk at 4:00 PM or 6:00 PM sharp, or when rooms become available due to nonarrivals.)

- If someone in your family travels for business, ask if you can use their corporate discount for use at chain hotels. Have business cards made up for your business. In many hotels all you have to do is show the card and you get a discount of at least 10%.
- When you pay on a weekly, monthly, or seasonal basis, the cost should be considerably less than that of daily accommodation. Bargain for better prices in these cases.

To save money when you make a room reservation, ask for a room by *price category* as minimum, standard or deluxe. If you want the minimum rate, ask for it. Ask for specials and what extras are included. Often, when you've reserved a minimum-rate room, and if none are available when you arrive, you will be upgraded to a better room at no additional cost.

When traveling with your family, try to stay where they offer a "family plan." Many hotels feature no charge or a nominal fee for a folding bed which can be set up in your room for children up to 18 years of age. Ask, as the age limits vary widely. Also, many hotels have special children's meal programs which can cut down on family food bills.

Tip: For a free list of budget hotels in the United States, send a self-addressed, stamped envelope to the American Hotel and Motel Association, 888 Seventh Avenue, New York, NY 10106. Many tourist offices also have these lists.

HOW TO SECURE
YOUR RESERVATION MONEY

I'm sure everyone has either personally experienced or heard some unfortunate friend tell of arriving at this or that hotel only to find that the reservation made two weeks or even two months ago has been lost. Once you have scouted around and made reservations—keeping in mind the above suggestions—there are some things the Frugal Traveler should know that will help him or her deal with such a situation, should it arise.

First, hotels are not required by the federal government to compensate guests whose reservations they cannot honor. Even if you have a written confirmation and have paid your bill in advance, a hotel is under no legal obligation to provide you with a room. The hotel is not even required to help you find another one elsewhere.

However, you can protect yourself from being turned away by a hotel by using the Assured Reservations Program now offered by all major charge and credit card companies. This is known in the industry as "guaranteed reservations." When making your reservation, give the hotel your credit card number in order to hold your room for the entire night. In general, as long as you call the hotel by 6 PM local time (4 PM at resort hotels), you can cancel a guaranteed reservation without penalty. Get your cancellation number in case the hotel bills your account.

Tip: Always be sure when making your reservation to ask for the cancellation time.

With a guaranteed reservation—if your hotel is oversold and it is participating in the Assured Reservations program—the hotel must provide you with a free room for one night at a comparable hotel, plus transportation to that hotel and one free long-distance phone call. Hotels not in that program may do the same, particularly if you complain loudly to the management in the hotel lobby and if you call the local tourist bureau with your complaint. Some will keep you at another hotel until they have an available room.

HOW YOU CAN STAY WITH THE RICH AND FAMOUS AND SOME OTHER ACCOMMODATION OPTIONS TO CONSIDER

When occupancy is down, even many of the best hotels in the world will advertise special rates. The best place to find these is in the Sunday travel section of major city newspapers like *The New York Times* and in magazines and newspapers in areas you will visit. Read the small type—these prices are often per person, double occupancy, exclusive of taxes and subject to availability. Check to make sure you can get the promotion the day of the week you need and check whether there is an expiration date or other restrictions.

The easiest way to cut hotel costs and stay at glamorous hotels is to buy your accommodations as part of a tour package. Not every hotel has a package, but so many do that you may have a large choice. Packages are arranged by wholesale tour operators and sold through retail travel agents, and some agencies specialize in better hotel properties. The tour operator can offer travelers prices substantially below the hotels' regular rates. The larger discounts are generally at the medium- and high-priced end of the spectrum, and many travelers are surprised to learn that in many cases the room available through a tour operator is much better than any the traveler could get on his own. This is because the agent may buy the room for the year, cutting costs dramatically. You'll never get these prices dealing directly with the hotel. In big cities, as we mentioned, major hotels promote weekend specials, about half price, and you can obtain these yourself just by calling and asking. Remember, single travelers may not find these packages bargains because of the single surcharge.

Tip: Many of even the best hotels have second-night-free programs. They are a real bargain if you're staying exactly two days and if there's a room available at that price. Be alert to the fact that the hotels may reserve the deluxe rather than the lowest-priced rooms for this and for the club programs. However, if you ask you can often get the category you want.

You might also get a discount on staying at the poshest places through travel clubs or other organizations. I know people who have stayed at very large discounts and even free at some of the best hotels in the world through their credit card promotions or special interest or travel clubs. For example, a popular credit card earned a friend a free flight to Paris and a free stay at a very posh Parisian hotel.

Join the Rich and Famous for Tea or Dinner or Dancing: Reserve a table at a restaurant you have always heard about, or stop by at a hotel or resort you have always dreamed of going to. You can always go in for the price of tea, ice cream or a drink at their lounge. You can see it all if you browse in their boutiques or take walks around the grounds.

Also, it is now very much in vogue to stop in to have dessert or tea in better restaurants, especially in major hotels. Here are some great places that now have official teatime in New York: the Carlyle Hotel Gallery, Helmsley Palace Gold Room, Mayfair Regent, and Pierre Hotel Rotunda. Tea is also served at the Plaza Hotel, Algonquin Oak Room, American Stanhope Tearoom, Inter-Continental Tearoom and Waldorf-Astoria Cocktail Terrace. And you may be able to use two-for-one coupons for meals at many of the better restaurants and hotels. I had dinner at the Arizona Biltmore, regarded as one of the 10 best hotels in the world, using a two-for-one-coupon, and got one meal free! I got this coupon from an offer in my last book, *The Frugal Shopper*.

Below is a partial listing of some of the super-deluxe hotels and resorts. This is where you can find celebrities and rub elbows with the rich and famous. You can eat there, browse, walk around, dance, or have tea.

The Ritz—Paris
The Beverly Hills Hotel—Los Angeles, CA
The Bel-Air Hotel—Los Angeles, CA
Claridges—London
Carlyle—New York
Pierre—New York
The Regent—Hong Kong
The Mandarin—Hong Kong
The Baur au Lac—Zurich
The Cipriani—Venice
The Oriental—Bangkok
The Vier Jahreszeiten—Hamburg
The Hassler—Rome
Grand Cyprus—Orlando, FL
Harrah's Lake Tahoe—Stateline, NV
Williamsburg Inn—Williamsburg, VA
Arizona Biltmore—Phoenix, AZ
The Registry—Scottsdale, AZ
Marriott's Camelback Inn—Scottsdale, AZ
Hyatt Regency—Scottsdale, AZ
The Wigwam—Litchfield Park, AZ

C Lazy U Ranch—Granby, CO
Tall Timber—Durango, CO
Boca Raton Hotel and Club—Boca Raton, FL
The Breakers—Palm Beach, FL
The Broadmoor—Colorado Springs, CO
The Cloister Sea Island—Sea Island, GA
Marriott's Rancho Las Palmas—Palm Springs, CA
Ritz-Carlton Laguna Niguel—Laguna Niguel, CA
Caesar Park Hotel—Rio de Janeiro
The Greenbrier—White Sulphur Springs, WV
The Homestead—Hot Springs, VA

SOME OTHER ACCOMMODATION OPTIONS

Not everyone wants to stay in a hotel, and there are some wonderful options available to the Frugal Traveler that I'd also like to mention.

You can sometimes pay less for more charm: When traveling, check out the mansions, private villas, restored older hotels or small, newer, local hotels, pensions, inns and guest houses—these are often available for less money. In smaller lodgings you'll be more likely to have contact with your hosts, because a family often runs them, and you'll likely receive helpful, honest advice on local restaurants, shops and sights. There's no better way to get to know a country or an area than by staying with a local person.

For the young at heart: In the US youth hostels are most frequently accessible and practical in areas of higher population density like New England. Although they are mostly used by younger people, there is no age limit; and in many hostels, during off-season, couples are often permitted to be the sole occupants of a dorm room. However, you must be a member to use the hostels. Write to American Youth Hostels, Inc., 1332 I St., N.W., Washington, DC 20005. A copy of the *Hostel Guide and Handbook* will be included in your membership.

Budget-minded travelers should also look for bargain accommodations at tourist homes or family-style YMCAs and YWCAs. There are Ys all over the world that offer clean, wholesome lodging. Check with local Ys for information. Some state and federal parks also provide inexpensive lodging. Hundreds of colleges offer dormitory accommodations to tourists during vacations at single-room rates of $2–$10 per night; with meals from $1–$5.

· 6 ·

Travel Advantages

for Singles, Couples,

Families,

and Senior Citizens

All kinds of people travel—young and old, singles, couples and families—and though we've been going over the many ways to get the best value for anyone who wants to become a Frugal Traveler, there are also many specific savings opportunities geared to particular travelers and travel groups. The single person has a certain flexibility the family doesn't, but the family can take advantage of special bargains unavailable to the single. In this chapter, I'd like to share with you some money-saving information concerning specific opportunities for those in special travel categories. These tips and ideas should be used alongside the general Frugal Traveler ideas we've spoken of up to now and, whether you yourself are young or not so young, single, part of a couple or part of a family, there should be something here for you. The Frugal Traveler is one on whom nothing, not even the slightest money-saving opportunity, is lost!

THE COUPLE: ENJOY ROMANTIC INTERLUDES ON ANY BUDGET

Honeymooners, whether on their first, second or third honeymoon—and other romantics—need to plan special trips which meet the needs, temperaments and budgets of the couple. How to find romance on any budget is an art in itself, and one that will really pay off.

Couples should plan travel together since how and where money is spent is usually the number one cause of arguments before, during, and after the trip. Couples have to decide on a budget for the vacation before they go. Do on vacation what you both like to do. If you're on a limited budget, try to plan your honeymoon or vacation in low season or right before or after the high season. The Loire Valley and other romantic spots have splendid scenery and can be admired at any time of the year. Save money while you enjoy. Try to avoid the crowds and extreme heat of July and August. Off-season, in May and June— when weddings are so popular—prices are lower and the areas are particularly attractive in spring. September is also a good month, with relatively fine weather and lower prices in many spots.

Tip: Camping is romantic and can be great fun whether you're on a budget or not. And staying at romantic inns in out of the way places is great for the budget and for love!

A cruise can be the ultimate romantic vacation on any budget. There are cruises to satisfy almost anyone, of any age, with different lifestyles, backgrounds and interests. So whatever your interest, there's a cruise for you. There are many different budget levels for cruises, and if you go to the correct source you have a good chance of finding one to fit your budget.

Staterooms vary from tight to luxurious sizes, and most everything is usually included. Pick a cabin in your budget and take a short or long cruise according to your time, interests and budget limitations.

Weekend Romance on any Budget: Take off for the weekend and make it to an offbeat, romantic, charming, tranquil, festive, exciting, active, luxurious destination, during quiet times or special events and festivals. Plan for picnicking, cultural and romantic evenings, and entertainment. You can do it on the most meager budget if you plan properly. Or spend the weekend in a posh hotel that offers two nights for the price of one, or go where there are inns and Bed & Breakfast guest houses for any budget. To economize, make yourselves a quiet candlelight dinner. Or splurge by eating in a candlelit restaurant! It's up to your budget and your desires!

Save Money on "Escape Weekends": You can stay within 125 miles of your home, go by car and enjoy special interests and lower transportation costs. Before departing, inquire about discounts.

Be sure to plan well in advance for an auto trip. Know your itinerary, and make reservations. Make sure your car is in good repair, as I mentioned, so your good times aren't spoiled.

Tip: The Wilderness Society operates all types of tours, from hiking, backpacking and canoeing to horseback riding, in wilderness areas throughout the US. Emphasis is on getting to know the wilderness in a nondestructive way. For information, write to the Wilderness Society, Western Regional Office, 4260 Evans Avenue, Denver, CO 80222.

Single and Looking for Romance?: Check newspapers for singles weekends and singles nights at hotels and retreats like the singles weekends at various resorts. I've known many a marriage match made at these gatherings! Also, check for singles cruises by calling the cruise lines.

FRUGAL FAMILY TRAVEL

Traveling is expensive, but even more so when a large family travels together. When traveling with the family costs multiply quickly, and money saving should be a prime concern. There are bargains around on all types of possible vacations and trips for all types of families, including camping, international and domestic travel, trips to luxury resorts, the "club" resorts and house exchanges.

Flying with Children:

Flying with Children: Usually a child under 2 years of age, not occupying a seat, flies free within the US and at a fare of 10% for international travel. A second infant without a second adult is charged the fare applicable to children ages 2–11. This is usually about 50% of an adult economy fare and two thirds of an adult APEX fare. On charters, children usually pay full fare. Check to see if the airline will provide you with a bassinet and request a bulkhead seat so you can use the space for it. Charter and some tour vacations can be much more expensive for a family because operators usually charge full fare and lodging for each person, children as well as adults.

Look for air/car promotions that benefit family travel. Many airlines are promoting a tie-in rental car for a week, with car rental costing not much more than airfare alone. You should consider this because you may need a car to get around with children. Check if the advertised price is per person, and requires a minimum of two people: Double the advertised price when you're comparison shopping for two of you, but there should be no extra charge for the rest of the family. Read the small print.

The promotional price usually applies only to the first week of rental. If you want to rent for more than a week, you may pay another rate. Ask!

Hotels: Some countries and local areas publish brochures and listings of one-star and two-star hotels, many of them family-operated, that are good for lower budget family travel. Newer facilities domestically and worldwide usually come with more amenities, including private baths. Some may charge less for a room with only hot and cold water sinks in the room and public toilets and showers. Get what you can afford.

Children are charged from nothing to half rate by many hotels, so ask for special rates when you book. Stay where they do not charge for children in your room. But be prepared to spend extra for a hotel that is suitable for children rather than a real budget lodging that you could use if you were traveling without children.

Cruises: Some cruise lines are well-equipped to handle young passengers only during holiday seasons. Be sure to select a line which caters to children. There are usually very substantial discounts for children who share a cabin with two full-fare adults.

For the Frugal Traveler with children, real preparation is needed. Remember to bring the necessities—food, medicine, clothing, and "security" items from home which will give children a sense of stability. As always, make advance reservations. Traveling with children can be wonderful or miserable, depending on how well parents plan. Keep them busy, and make frequent stops!

Some Money-Saving Family Vacations: Discover the fun of the great outdoors with your family. And remember, you can take more luggage and make more purchases en route if you have a car. A family travels with no increase in ground transportation costs above what the parents would spend traveling alone. You can go camping, hunting, fishing and boating or you can just plain have a good time in a local recreation area—either one can be economical for a large or small family. Guest ranches and farms offer a wide variety of activities. There are conventional as well as varied and unusual types of activities available for family travel. A package tour, or renting a house, is sometimes an easy and economical way to plan a family vacation experience. Ask a travel agent for details.

Home Exchange: Vacations through home-exchanging—anywhere in the world—can make a family vacation dream a real bargain as well. You save on lodging costs, use their laundry and recreational facilities, and even their car. Home exchange also gives you a chance to meet local people, learn their language and culture.

You can find out about home exchanges through major newspapers (domestic and foreign), local telephone books, community host organizations, colleges and universities, international associations, and travel books on the subject.

THE SINGLE

Singles, students and youth can now travel for less—sometimes even free—and enjoy travel more than ever before.

For singles and student travelers there is a whole world out there just waiting and willing to provide you with options for bargain travel and huge savings. You have many terrific options. If you have ideas on unique travel, find out more from specialized travel agents, your local and school library, your school guidance counselor, tourist and government offices, and local and religious organizations. Sometimes friends and older siblings and their friends who have benefited from certain travel experiences are the best resources for travel ideas.

Youth fares and student fares have varied age cutoffs, usually anywhere from 21 to 26 years of age. When applicable, they can save you a great deal of money. However, as with senior programs, always ask for other promotional fares besides the student fares. Although these are usually among the best prices, sometimes there are better deals available for a particular traveler at a particular time.

Some tours on most cruise lines will arrange to provide singles with a roommate. The single surcharge varies from 10 to 75%, and the average single supplement runs 50% above the per-person rate. Some cruise lines will allow singles to travel alone in a cabin, at no extra cost, when they know a ship won't be full. Ask! Many facilities that cater to singles try to avoid charging supplements for lone travel through various arrangements. This can make a big difference in what singles can afford. Also, some hotels and cruise lines offer discounts to a third or fourth person who shares the same room or cabin with two paying the regular rate. Ask!

If you're under 26 years of age, traveling through Europe, a Eurail pass can be a good deal, depending on how much and where you'll be traveling. But you must travel second class and pay a surcharge for express trains, and the pass must be purchased before leaving the US. In Europe, youth hostels are widely available, and prices are reasonable.

In France, a special youth card offering discounts on air and rail transportation as well as admission to sporting and cultural events is available to people 25 years old and under. The Carte Jeune, or Youth Card, is good for some big discounts during specified times at many hotels, and for some air and rail travel and at some restaurants and sporting events. The card grants access to university dining rooms, where meal costs are low, and to university dormitories during summer vacation, at very inexpensive rates per night. The card is sold to visitors aged 25 and under at town halls, tourist offices, and at Credit Mutuel banks.

Tip: There are student fees or reduced-price passes for most tourist attractions. Ask if discount is not posted. And whether or not you are a student, the presentation of an International Student ID card with your picture attached will get you discounts on some transport and lodging.

Also, leave your itinerary with friends and relatives so they will be able to reach you.

For single people who don't wish to travel alone, or pay big supplements, contact either the National Partners Club, Inc., Suite 210-A, 7135 SR 52, Hudson, FL 33567, or the Travel Companion Exchange, P.O. Box 833, Amityville, NY 11701.

Also, a group of nine student organizations in Europe offers 15–30% reductions on point-to-point Eurotrain rail tickets (reduction rates depend on the distance traveled). In the US you can get a voucher for these Eurotrain tickets from the International Study and Travel Center 91STCO, 44 Coffman Memorial Union, 300 Washington Ave., SE, University of Minnesota, Minneapolis, MN 55455 (612-373-0180).

Also, check the often inexpensive overland possibility of bus travel all over the world. Check the price, quality and quantity of the service offered. Magic Bus offers cheap, direct bus service between major cities in Europe. Miracle Bus and Magic Tours' Budget Bus are other reasonable coach services running between major cities. For information, contact their offices in the US at 1745 Clement, San Francisco, CA 94121.

Important: Student travelers should get the previously mentioned International Student ID Card for discounts at museums, concerts, theaters, and on youth rail and boat passes. Also, the 5- or 10-day Youth Travelcard, good for unlimited bus travel, is really a bargain. It is available through travel agents in the US and on InterEuropean student charter flights. To get the I.S.I Card, apply to the Council on International Educational Exchange, 205 East 42 St., New York, NY 10017, or 312 Sutter St., San Francisco, CA 94108. Canadian students should apply to the Association of Student Councils, 44 St. George St. Toronto, ON M5S, QE4.

There are a number of travel agencies specializing in student travel, but many push very expensive tours so check for good prices. Write to: Intercollegiate Holidays, Inc., 501 Madison Avenue, New York, NY 10022, or Suite 18, 1007 Broxton Ave., Los Angeles, CA 90024 (the official representative of the U.S. National Student Association and the National Student Travel Bureau).

Finally, these are many money-saving student and youth programs that give good value. Some are open to people of all ages. The programs, however, are not suitable for everyone. Programs, prices, facilities and personnel change often, so you should check and know all details before you go. The following agencies offer various types of programs:

Arista Student Travel Assoc., 1 Rockefeller Plaza, New York, NY 10020.

American International Student Exchange, 77 Lookout Drive, La Jolla, CA 92037, 619-459-9761.

American Youth Hostels, National Administrative Offices, 13321 I Street NW, Suite 800, Washington, DC 20005, 202-738-6161. Open to everyone regardless of age. Membership fees entitle you to inexpensive accommodations at over 5,000 hostels worldwide, travel information, and educational programs.

Canadian Hosteling Association, 333 River Road, Canter City, Ottawa, K1L 8B9 Canada.

Education Foundation for Foreign Study, 1528 Chapala Street, Santa Barbara, CA 93101, 805-963-0553.

International Christian Youth Exchange, 134 W. 26 St., New York, NY 10001, 212-206-7307.

American Zionist Youth Foundation, 515 Park Ave., New

York, NY 10022, 212-751-6070. Has excellent summer programs in Israel for both high school age and college age. Programs include touring, kibbutz visit, study, sports and arts.

Tips: Inexpensive student accommodations are frequently available on college campuses during school recesses. Check on availability before you go.

Some airlines allow you to take a bicycle or other athletic equipment instead of one piece of your luggage allowance. Consider this when you are figuring the cost of your total airfare as other airlines may charge extra.

THE FRUGAL SENIOR CITIZEN CAN ENJOY IT ALL

Senior citizens can travel all over the world and get huge savings. However, finding the best bargains for the senior Frugal Traveler requires careful evaluation of the many discounts, programs and clubs available to senior citizens, and this section, therefore, is must reading for seniors.

Throughout the world senior citizens are eligible for big discounts on almost every form of transportation. Be sure you have identification with you at all times, so that you will not miss out on the savings. In some cases you need to belong to a certain club or organization. Call the clubs' 800-numbers and ask!

Airlines and all major transportation systems and most hotel chains offer programs that grant senior travelers unlimited travel with the payment of a set fee, or sometimes no fee at all. Senior passes of this type abound.

The Following Are Some Suggestions That Will Greatly Benefit Many Seniors: Participants in Elder hostels sleep in college dorms and eat in the school cafeterias. You can learn, and have a terrific vacation, at the same time. Elderhostel, for 60-plus seniors, has more than 17,000 programs in the US and Canada, and 3,000 programs abroad. Elderhostel offers room, board, and six days of courses at various colleges at bargain prices. For more information and a catalog, write to Elderhostel, 80 Boylston St., Suite 400, Boston, MA 02116.

- For people 50 years and older, Grand Circle has trips for solo travelers; these trips provide you with no-fee traveler's checks, free travel insurance, advancement of medical costs in case of emergency and a representative to assist travelers at the airport. Grand Circle also gets seniors special discounts, slower paced itineraries, and Saga special services, like the Saga Holidays Travel MedCard, a wallet-sized plastic card containing a microfilm chip on which the traveler's medical history is entered. Saga also offers special grandparents and grandchildren holidays, on which travelers can be accompanied by children aged 6–16.

- For seniors 62 years of age or older, free admission to all national parks and federal recreation areas can be obtained with a Golden Age Passport, which also entitles seniors to a 50% discount on camping fees. Write to: Golden Age Card, National Parks Services, C and 19th Streets, NW, Washington, DC 20006, 202-343-7394.

- Members of the American Association of Retired Persons (annual dues, $5) and other organizations for seniors can get discounts at several chains of hotels. In some cases, seniors get better prices buying a nonseason discounted tour package. Investigate each deal separately.

- Finally, to attract seniors, some airlines and other public transits offer several types of discounts for the elderly. Call the airlines', railroads', and bus lines' 800-numbers to get information on senior discount programs. You can call Amtrak at 800-872-7245 for a train price quote and, for buses, Greyhound has discounts if you are 65 or older, and Trailways at 212-730-7460, offers a 10% discount.

TRAVEL INFORMATION FOR HANDICAPPED TRAVELERS

There are wonderful tours for the physically handicapped. Just be certain that the one you've selected is the suitable pace and price for you. Get out and enjoy life with others. There are special camps and funds available through government and private agencies to help you pay for vacations. Some sources of information are:

- Rehabilitation International, 1123 Broadway, New York, NY 10010, publishes a 16-page *International Directory of Access Guides*—a bibliography of 275 individual manuals of access possibilities at travel facilities all over the US, Canada, and European countries.
- Valuable information about motels, hotels, and restaurants (rating them, detailing steps, table heights, etc.) can be found in *Where Turning Wheels Stop,* published by Paralyzed Veterans of America, 3636 16th St., NW, Washington, DC 20000, as well as The Wheelchair Traveler, by Douglar R. Annand, Ball Hill Rd., Milford, NH 03055.
- Many of the nation's national parks have special facilities for the handicapped. These are in the *National Park Guide for the Handicapped,* available from the US Government Printing Office, Washington, DC 20402.
- Access To The World, 2828 E. Colfax Avenue, Denver, CO 80206.
- Flying Wheels Travel, 143 W. Bridge, Owatonna, MN 55060.
- Mobility International U.S.A., P.O. Box 3551, Eugene, OR 97403.
- Wheelchair Wagon Tours, P.O. Box 1270, Kissimmee, FL 32742.
- Access Travel: A free booklet that specifies facilities and services at airport terminals worldwide. Write to Consumer Information Center, Pueblo, CO 81009.
- *The Handicapped Drivers Mobility Guide* is free to AAA members. Write to AAA Traffic Safety Dept., 8111 Gatehouse Road, Falls Church, VA 22047.
- Wheels On Tour, Inc., 2020 Cohasset, Canoga Park, CA 91306.
- TWA publishes a free 12-page pamphlet entitled *Consumer Information About Air Travel For The Handicapped*.
- You can get information from the Easter Seal Society for

Crippled Children and Adults. Write to the Director of Education and Information Service, 2023 West Ogden Avenue, Chicago, IL 50512.

- Greyhound's Helping Hand program for handicapped bus travelers allows disabled persons to be accompanied by a traveling companion at no extra charge. Call for a brochure.
- A booklet called *Access Amtrak: A Guide to Amtrak Services for Elderly Handicapped Travelers,* is available free of charge. Write to Amtrak Public Affairs, 400 North Capitol St., NW, Washington, DC 20001.
- In Britain, the Royal Association for Disability and Rehabilitation, is the principal source for all information on handicapped travel. They produce an excellent, annually updated guide called *Holidays for the Physically Handicapped.* Write to 25 Mortimer St., London W.1. Other countries and local areas have similar source material. Contact Offices of Tourism in each locality of interest.
- *Cruise Guide for the Wheelchair Traveler.* Write Cruise Lines International, 17 Battery Place, Suite 631, New York, NY 10004. Free of charge.
- Disabled travelers should also check with large transit systems and airlines worldwide for special discounts.
- For Braille travel books write to Braille Institute Press, 741 N. Vermont Ave., Los Angeles, CA 90029.

Disclaimer: This list is for your information and investigation, but is not a recommendation of these sources.

INFORMATION ON MONEY-SAVING TRAVEL SOURCES FOR FRUGAL TRAVELERS OF ALL AGES AND INTERESTS

What follows is a list of sources of information which, unlike those in the earlier part of this chapter, are not organized according to specific situations. Rather, I've decided to throw them all together in the hope that the Frugal Traveler may be exposed to some sources he or she wouldn't have otherwise been aware of. I hope that these sources may spark a new, different and truly memorable Frugal Traveler vacation!

AARP American Association of Retired Persons, 1909 K Street, NW, Washington, DC 20049, 202-872-4700. Specialties: Group programs for retired people. Cost: Varies. Countries: Worldwide.

The American Hiking Society, Volunteer Vacations, P.O. Box 86, North Scituate, MA 02060. Specialty: Volunteer work restoring and building trails and bridges. Registration fee. Country: US.

American International Student Exchange, 7728 Lookout Drive, La Jolla, CA 92037, 619-459-9761. Educational programs abroad. Cost. Worldwide travel.

Bicycle USA, Suite 2009, 6707 Whitestone Road, Baltimore, MD 21207, 301-944-3399. Specialties: Homestays, travel information, educational programs, recreation and referrals to local bicycle clubs for cyclists. Membership fee required. Country: US.

Council Travel Services West, 1093 Broxton Avenue, Los Angeles, CA 90024. Specialties: Information on working and studying abroad. Cost: Varies. Countries: Great Britain, France, Germany and New Zealand.

Cyclists' Touring Club, 69 Meadrow, Godalming, Durrey, England 004868-7217. Specialties: Operating bicycling tours worldwide with an emphasis on the British Isles and Europe. Cost: Varies. Countries: Worldwide.

Earthwatch, 10 Juniper Road, Belmont, MA 02178, 617-489-3030. Specialties: Scientific expeditions. Cost: Varies. Countries: Worldwide.

The Globetrotters Club, BCM/Roving, London WCIN 3XX England. In the US, call 818-352-2469. Specialty: Budget travel information. Countries: Worldwide.

Holiday Exchanges, Box 5294, Ventura, CA 93003, 805-642-4879. Specialties: Subscription service for holiday exchanges, rentals, house-sitting and mutual hospitality.

Home Exchange International, Inc., 22458 Ventura Boulevard, Suite E, Woodland Hills, CA 91367, 818-992-8990. Specialty: Personalized exchange of homes for vacations or sabbaticals between the US, Europe and Israel.

Interhostel, University of New Hampshire, Division of Continuing Education, 6 Garrison Avenue, Durham, NH 03824, 603-862-1147. Specialties: Promotes international understanding and goodwill and continuing education of older adults. The age requirement is usualy from 50 to 65, and many programs permit a companion of any age to travel with the senior at the same discounted fare. Low cost tuition.

International Home Exchange Service/INTERVACK US, P.O. 3975, San Francisco, CA 94119, 415-382-0300. Specialties: Home exchanges and visits. Membership required.

Interservice Home Exchange, Box 87, Glen Echo, MD 20812, 301-229-7567. Specialty: Temporary exchange of homes for purposes of vacations and business travel in the US and abroad.

National Council of Senior Citizens, 925 15th Street, NW, Washington, DC 20005. Specialty: Travel information for senior citizens on discount lodging, dining and transportation.

National 4H Council, 7100 Connecticut Avenue, Washington, D.C. 20015, 301-656-9000. Specialties: Agricultural programs for youth.

National Park Service, U.S. Dept. of the Interior, Washington, DC 20240. Specialties: Volunteers in national parks.

Peace Corps, Washington, DC 20525. Specialties: Community work in developing nations.

Touring Cyclists' Directory, 13623 Sylvan, Van Nuys, CA 91401, 818-781-5865. Specialty: Lists overnight accommodations for cyclists. The program is reciprocal: you must offer a bed and shower in exchange for your stays. Cost: None. A small contribution, however, is welcomed.

United States Student Travel Service, 801 Second Avenue, New York, NY 10017, 212-867-8770. Specialties: Travel services, information, homestays, education, low-cost flights, special interest tours and summer jobs.

United States Tour and Travel Exchange, Barterbrook Square, Staunton, VA 24401. Specialties: Exchange of personal tours. Cost: Little or none.

Vacation Exchange Club, Inc., 12005 11th Avenue, Unit 12, Youngstown, AZ 85363, 602-972-2186. Specialties: Rent-free or other money-saving vacations. Also, home exchange, rent, hospitality, exchanges, bed and breakfast, exchange of boats or cars, country clubs, etc. Cost: Two issues of The Exchange Book cost $15. Countries: Canada, US, Mexico, Caribbean, Australia, New Zealand, United Kingdom and Mexico.

VISIT/USA, 356 West 34th Street, New York, NY 10001, 212-760-5856. Specialty: Low-cost accommodations. A program of the YMCA, this international service and membership organization offers safe, inexpensive stays. Cost: Low. Countries: Worldwide.

Whole Person Tours, Inc., P.O. Box 1084, Bayonne, NJ 07002-1084, 201-858-3400. Specialty: Tours for the disabled.

Disclaimer: Author and publisher do not vouch for or guarantee services or claims of groups mentioned in this book, nor accept any responsibility for transactions which may result from publishing this information, assumed to be accurate at the time of publication. All information is subject to change.

· 7 ·

Special Opportunities

Available to the Business

and Frequent Traveler

Business and frequent travelers can save enormous sums of money with free trips and fringe benefits— and even get money back—if they know some of the ins and outs of travel. For these frequent flyers and business people it pays to keep track of the changing programs and rules and requirements in order to take maximum advantage of the airline, hotel, car rental and credit card companies' travel offers.

There are little-known secrets that can save money and increase the success, convenience and comfort of the business traveler and frequent traveler. There are many special bargains out there for these travelers; you can qualify for many special clubs, join organizations and be solicited by all major travel-related businesses for your valuable patronage. But you must learn how to select the best hotel clubs, auto clubs, airline clubs, and credit card clubs to meet your specific needs, concentrating only on those that give you the best value. Frequently you will get mail with offers for discounts that others are not aware of because your name appears on special "big spender" mailing lists. You should pay attention to these because often an offer that comes in the mail may be terrific for you.

In deciding on the best credit card to carry, as well as which clubs and organizations you, as a frequent or business traveler, should belong to, check with friends in a similar financial position and business associates or highly qualified travel agents who specialize in servicing business people. These people are usually the best sources of information. Benefit from the experience of others and find out which options you have, which have benefited others financially and which have provided them with the best services and conveniences. Others can suggest ways you may never have thought of that will greatly increase your frequent traveler benefits. Other sources of information are travel magazines and the Sunday travel section of your newspaper, radio and TV-business programs and ads. Many frequent flyers and those who stay in hotels frequently, and those who run up big totals on their credit cards for business and personal spending, have learned that they can use these as financial assets to save thousands of dollars, both on vacations for themselves and their families, and for free or better business travel in the future. There are techniques that some frequent travelers have developed that enable them to travel to all the best vacation spots free, or almost free, and to fly first class at coach prices or less. You need to know which airlines, hotels, credit cards or car rental companies offer the best deals so that you can get these benefits, too.

Business travelers, like other travelers, can save money by booking air space in advance, thereby getting the discount rates available to all travelers who book in advance. The problem most business travelers experience, however, is that they often have to travel by air at the last minute. For routes you will fly frequently, find out what the benefits are on all the airlines that service that route, and select the same airline each time you fly to accumulate valuable frequent flyer bonus awards.

Ask if there are stand-by fares for when you want to fly if you find you can't book in advance. Be aware that on certain airlines you save nothing for the stand-by fare. On some airlines, standby may be a real bargain, while on others it is the full, undiscounted price. You could, however, get first-class seats on some airlines for bargain prices, if that is all that is available in standby. Remember that options vary with each carrier. Once abroad, you get the same services as others in your area of the plane. Sometimes standby is the most expensive category available. Even at the last minute always see if you can purchase a cheaper category.

The frugal business traveler makes sure everything goes as smoothly as possible, even if the initial costs seem higher; it is penny-wise and dollar-foolish to spend all your time, energy and money to travel to see a business contact and spoil things because of a lack of proper preparation and planning or because of penny-pinching.

Frugal business travelers spend what is economically feasible to get the most from a business trip. On some trips, where you will need to bring people to your hotel, or make an impression, it may be important to pay for a suite in a posh hotel, while on another trip the same traveler may be able to get by in a budget motel. Look for the best values according to your needs. Remember, being frugal never means being cheap.

CASHING IN FOR FREQUENT TRAVELERS

Often frequent-flyer programs really pay off. They have millions of enrollees—anyone who flies often ought to consider joining at least one, and possibly several, of these programs. The programs offer various awards to enrolled members based on accumulated mileage on the airline or other affiliated airlines. Awards can range from a free upgrade to unlimited, free, system-wide travel. Many programs offer awards that include travel benefits for the members' spouses in addition to those for the members themselves, and frequent travelers can sell extra tickets they accumulate. Signing up is free in all except a few cases. Fill out an application that you can get at an airline ticket counter—just for joining, you usually get free mileage credits. The programs offer fabulous bonuses—the average award is worth about $500, and the airlines gave out an estimated $100 million worth of prizes last year.

The following are things to keep in mind for those looking into frequent flyer bonus programs:

- Frequent flyers should not be lured into overspending to qualify for a prize.
- Determine whether the mileage credits are worth the money you are spending. Many hotels connected to frequent-flyer plans are simply too expensive for many limited budgets.
- Hotel and motel chains have frequent-guest plans. Guests can earn prizes, including free cruises, air travel, rental cars and hotel stays, savings bonds, appliances, etc.
- By raising prize levels and then allowing flyers unlimited time in which to earn credits sufficient to claim a particular prize, carriers are attempting to get you into their programs. The trick is to get you to fly just a few more miles on their airline in order to get the prize you really want—beware.
- Pay attention to using your bonuses before the expiration date, after which you lose the full benefits.
- Many airlines are becoming strict about allowing customers to transfer their children or business associates. It is smart, therefore, to keep aware of changing restrictions and cash in on awards before the restrictions are so limited that you lose your benefits.
- Save all travel receipts until you receive a statement confirming your frequent bonus credits.
- Increasingly, corporations are discouraging employees from running up big bonus allotments for themselves if it means extra expense to employers. Investigate your employer's policies on and attitudes about these plans, or you could jeopardize your job.
- Look for programs which have guaranteed reward levels that have long-term guaranteed dates to cash in.
- Look for programs which have the lowest reward levels and can get you rewards quickly.

Special Opportunities for the Business and Frequent Traveler

When you fly a lot, look for programs that have tie-ins or specials that you can use as extras that include the awarding of bonus miles for traveling specific routes, for renting cars from participating agencies, for staying at hotels that participate with the airlines and for flying on commuter or foreign airlines participating in the program. You can learn of new or changing tie-ins and specials by reading the free newsletters that the airlines send to all frequent-flyer program enrollees.

- Enroll in the plans of the one or two carriers that fly to places you travel to most often.
- In choosing a program, consider how accurately the airline tracks the mileage credits you've accumulated and how often it tells you the amount you've earned. An airline that totals your mileage electronically as you buy your ticket, best keeps errors to a minimum. Keep verifiable records of everything that adds to your total. All the airlines send program participants periodic statements on which your most recent mileage credits are itemized and added to the amounts earned earlier.

Some Secrets of Very Successful Bonus Collecting

- Divide a long trip into segments instead of flying nonstop, as each segment often brings extra mileage credits. On some routes, bonuses are very high.
- Rent a car one day, turn it in in 24 hours, and take out another one. Each rental can bring extra credit. Rent a luxury car instead of a compact if you get enough bonus miles to warrant it, as in competitive markets where this increases rewards. Make certain that any extra costs you might incur are acceptable to your own business or your boss's budgets.
- Check in and out of the same hotel (you don't actually have to lose the room) or change hotels repeatedly during a long stay in a particular city. In many hotels, just checking in earns the extra credits, no matter how long you stay. In many hotels, it is the cost of your room that earns the credits.

- Join reward programs where, during your stay in a hotel, everything you charge in the hotel earns you points— including money spent for your room, what you spend in the boutiques, coffee shops and restaurants, and room service.
- Pay for everything you can with a credit card that earns you bonuses for everything you charge, including plane tickets, food, clothes, etc.
- Book through companies participating in tie-in-programs with multiple and easy-to-use carriers, hotels, car-rental firms and cruise-ship lines. Airlines offer travelers many ways to earn bonus mileage, and major carriers have increasingly tied their frequent-flyer programs to those of other major airlines. Join in the bonus programs of those with ties with more than one airline for maximum benefits.
- Book through domestic airlines with few or no overseas routes that have tie-ins with one or more international carriers.
- Several large international airlines are now tie-in-partners with US airlines that have frequent-flyer bonus programs. Fly them.
- During peak-traveling periods, most carriers restrict or prohibit the use of awards. Fly when you can get *and* use the awards.
- Carriers often grant a great deal more mile bonuses to first-class and business-class passengers. Some give big bonus mileage for flying on new routes and for flying during off-peak periods. It may pay to utilize these bonus opportunities.

Prestige Programs: On some airlines, as we have seen, mileage credits earn you free travel or ticket upgrade, and other prizes. The prestige plans are for very frequent flyers, cost nothing to enroll in and enable you to take advantage of a variety of privileges that are unavailable or costly for other flyers. Among the benefits are favored treatment, round-trip tickets to any point and free upgrades to first class, upgrades from coach to first class for only a small price, use of unpublicized toll-free numbers to call in the event of baggage or ticketing problems, express check-in privileges and extra mileage credits. People in the prestige programs may also get additional tie-ins with selected US and foreign carriers, which can earn them even more extra bonus points.

You will usually be notified by the airline when you qualify for a prestige program.

Hotels: It is usually to the benefit of a frequent traveler to book a hotel that offers the frequent-stay hotel programs. Most of them now base awards on the dollars you've spent and, if it is okay with your employer, booking the best rooms, ordering from room service and taking business contacts to dinner in your hotel, will get you more of the freebies. Check your company's policy on awards. Your employer may want you to stay at designated, lower-cost hotels and/or use your bonuses for later business trips.

To make sure you cash in on bonus awards before their time limit expires, or before the promotion is dropped, apply the points to yourself and to members of your immediate family— there's no hotel resale market like the one for frequent-flyer airline coupons.

In general, keep records. It's the frugal thing to do. Make them simple, and keep them up to date. Make entries as you spend money or else you will forget to record many expenses. This can make a difference as to whether you will get frequency awards, whether you will be reimbursed for your expenses by your employer and whether you can get a tax reduction for your business expenses. Remember to keep a record for your employer *and* for the Internal Revenue Service. Paying by a company or personal check, or credit card, is a good record.

Cutting Phone Costs When Traveling: Next year, approximately 11 million Americans will travel overseas. Of those who travel on business or pleasure, nearly two-thirds will call home at least once while away. Many travelers will place their calls from their hotel rooms and many will be ripped off. The following are some important tips you should remember to save money on telephone charges while traveling.

- Use credit cards to give you records for verification of business expenses for tax deductions. Get a credit card if you don't already have one—you'll need it for frequent traveling.
- With some long-distance telephone services you can call from locations other than your home phone without paying extra. If you travel and use the phone a lot, check these services out.
- Avoid making collect, third-party or person-to-person calls. There is often a big charge for each such "operator-assisted" call. Carry your phone book to avoid paying for directory-assistance calls.
- Keep calls short. In some areas (like New York City) message units are charged for local calls—the longer you talk, the more you'll pay. If you can, call during off-peak hours when charges go down.

Telephone Tips Abroad: Hotels usually add charges to every call you make out of the hotel, and these surcharges vary from hotel to hotel and from country to country. Before you make any call from your hotel room, whether local, inside the country or international, ask about these surcharges.

Before we conclude this chapter, I would like to suggest one final point to the business or otherwise frequent traveler: consider developing a relationship with a large travel agency with a business clientele. Frequent travelers can benefit greatly by establishing a relationship with agencies that belong to one of the big business consortiums. They have a better chance at getting discounts at the more expensive, business-oriented hotels. Most of these agencies are large, and have access to airline arrangements that bend airline rules and modify restrictions. Increasingly, these agencies are handling discount tickets obtained through a consolidator, and they can get you good discounts on cruises and tours, too. My advice, then, would be to see if you can locate one or more of these consortium-agency offices convenient to your home or office, and check it out to see if it might be for you. Good luck!

▪ 8 ▪

Travel Emergencies -

How to Avoid

and Handle Them

So you don't hear yourself saying on your vacation, "I never thought this could happen to me!" I'd like to talk about travel problems and emergencies. This chapter should help you to avoid many unwanted surprises and expenses ranging from awful annoyances to devastating crises, as well as a host of other problems that can arise on a trip and spoil it. Such situations may threaten your health, safety, and welfare, and if you run into trouble in these areas your pocketbook may be likely to suffer. The Frugal Traveler takes precautions. If the precautions fail to prevent certain problems and emergencies, the Frugal Traveler has *anticipated* events and knows what to do to eliminate or alleviate the situation. What follows will mean a lot in terms of saving you time, energy, and money, and will help you become a Frugal Traveler even in the heat of troubled times.

TAKE PRECAUTIONS WITH CHARTERS

Make checks for deposits and payments out directly to an escrow account so the charter operator cannot spend your money until your flight, in both directions, and other tour travel has been completed. Before making out any checks, investigate the charter company. Make sure the charter company is bonded. Book through an accredited agent.

BEWARE OF TRAVEL SCAMS

Increasingly travel scams are becoming a national problem for innocent victims. If you receive a telephone call or mail promising you a "bonus" or a "free" or unrealistically inexpensive vacation, be wary, and don't take it. Do not give your credit card number out to telephone solicitors or to persons unknown to you. Do not be rushed or pressured into making hasty travel decisions or paying cash. Trust your instincts if you sense a fraud. Check references and consult with authorities, well-known carriers and professional organizations before you sign up or spend money for any trip. Don't buy from anyone who requires you to buy anything to qualify for the trip.

LOST LUGGAGE

Lost luggage is a problem faced by many flyers. It can cause a crisis or, at the very least, extreme annoyance. There are ways you can cut down on the possible loss of many of your belongings.

- Pack only items you absolutely need. Leave cherished items and valuables, as well as important papers, at home or in your carryon.
- Remove all tags from previous flights from your luggage and put your name and address (use a business address whenever possible; if you don't have one perhaps you can use that of a friend or relative) on the inside as well as on the outside of the bags.

- Put a copy of your itinerary inside each bag, so the airline can find you and return your luggage to you if it is recovered while you are still away.
- Allow sufficient time between planes on connecting flights for the transfer of your baggage from one plane to the other. Ask the airline, your travel agent, or consult The Official Airline Guide (OAG) for minimum connecting time.
- Keep important medical prescriptions and records, as well as eyeglasses, in your carryon.

It can take up to one year for an airline to declare that your baggage is officially lost, so reimbursements for losses can be a long time in coming.

In the event your luggage is lost you will be asked to produce receipts for the value of the suitcase and its contents if you ask for money for the lost luggage, from the airline. If you paid for the items with a credit card, companies keep statement records for up to six years, so this will help.

If a checked bag does not arrive on the same flight as the traveler, it is considered delayed until the airline decides it is lost. This can take months. When a bag is delayed, ask the airline to deliver it to you. Most airlines will comply with your request.

Always report to the airline and fill out forms for damaged luggage and missing bags *before you leave the airport*. Get a receipt for the claim check for the damaged or lost luggage. Do not sign any settlement papers.

Keep a list of lost baggage contents, and the receipts for purchasing new luggage and new contents both for the airline and for insurance claims. The airline will only be responsible for losses up to $1250 per person for domestic flights and $9 per pound per person for international travel. You must prove the value of items lost. Items that are not new will not be reimbursed for full value. Airlines do not usually reimburse for loss of furs, cash, jewelry, stereos, cameras, art, documents, fragile and other theft-prone items.

It's smart to buy the standard luggage-insurance policy sold by most travel agencies. It's also smart to check your homeowner's policy to see if it fully covers your valuables while you are traveling. Either leave your valuables in a bank safe-deposit box at home, or if you take any, pack them in your carry-on baggage.

Also, as previously mentioned, do not use your home address on your luggage. If you have a business address, use that instead. There are burglary rings that work airports worldwide, and they take addresses found on the outside of travelers' bags and inform contacts that you are traveling. Since your house may be empty, your home may be a prime burglary target.

Lock your luggage to prevent it from being easily opened. Luggage locks cannot prevent theft, but they can discourage it, since a thief would rather go for luggage with no protection. Locks can also protect your things from falling out of a bag that accidentally opens.

Protect important documents as you would cash. Make sure you have the serial numbers of passports, driver's licenses, insurance policies, traveler's checks, credit cards, transportation tickets, etc. In case of loss, these will make tracing and/or restoration of the documents much easier. Keep one copy with you and one copy at home with someone you can contact in an emergency—making at least these two photocopies is the best preparation.

Complaints?: First attempt to work out baggage claims with the airline. Call their Customer Relations department after you leave the airport. They will often do more for you than airport personnel. If you get insufficient satisfaction, call the Consumer Affairs Division, at 202-366-2220, or write Consumer Affairs Division, U.S. Department of Transportation, Suite 10405, 400 7th Street, SW, Washington, DC 20590—and include a daytime telephone number.

LOST PLANE TICKETS: HOW TO SAVE TIME AND MONEY IF YOU LOSE YOUR AIRLINE TICKET

The worst thing you can do is pay with cash. Buy your tickets with a credit card. If the lost ticket has been charged to a credit card you have your cardholder's receipt and can identify yourself, the airline supervisor at the airport may authorize issuance of a replacement ticket without charge. If the airline has the card number, it can verify by computer that the passenger claiming the loss is the same person to whom the ticket was sold. If the airline has the ticket number, it can alert personnel to watch for attempted illegal use.

For international flight tickets, if the lost ticket was bought with a credit card, and if the ticket number is available at check-in time, airlines will usually issue a replacement ticket without charge.

If a ticket has been purchased from a travel agent rather than directly from the airline, it is usually easier to obtain a replacement without paying additional fare. If, however, a lost ticket for a domestic flight was purchased for cash, directly from the airlines, you usually have to buy a replacement (because no record of the ticket number is available at the sales office or the airport check-in counter after 24 hours from purchase time). In this event you should fill out a "lost ticket refund application" and, up to four months later, the cost of the lost ticket is refunded if the ticket has not been used.

Important: Always keep a record of your ticket number so you can supply it immediately to the airline if you lose your ticket.

DRIVING?

Be aware that there are age minimums and maximums for car rentals. Minimum ages vary from 18 to 30, and maximum ages are often around 70. Before you leave, check out what legal licenses and other documents you are required to have to be legally able to drive in any particular country. You may need an International Driver's License.

Can you reduce insurance payments? Know what your regular insurance policies cover so that you don't buy extra insurance costs associated with travel. But make sure your insurance covers you sufficiently. I always advise getting extra insurance to make sure you are covered—if in doubt, always pay for the extra insurance. For example, Collision Damage Waiver Insurance (CDWI) is an expensive necessity without which you could have thousands of dollars added to your charges if there is any damage to a rental car.

TRAVELING HEALTHY

Hygienic conditions in many places are bad, so take particular care. Visitors should consult their doctor before departure and ask if any injections are needed against measles, tetanus, cholera, typhus, poliomyelitis, hepatitis, yellow fever, malaria or lesser-known "exotic" diseases. It is advisable to take your international vaccination certificate with you.

Observe good eating habits. Where water is unsafe, buy bottled water, and while some restaurants will tell you they serve boiled or bottled water, make certain that it really is. Also, if you are planning to drink boiled water in mountainous regions, remember that it must be boiled longer at higher elevations to kill parasites. Eat cooked vegetables and peel fresh fruit. Purifier tablets widely used in the US will not kill certain harmful bacteria. Of the more than 200 countries in the world, less than one-quarter have water that is safe for Americans to drink. Make it a rule that you do not drink the water unless you know the water is safe for you. Always use boiled or bottled water, even to brush teeth. If the water is not safe, often milk, ice cream or other dairy products in the country are probably not safe either.

When in doubt about any food or its sources, do without.

Better safe than sorry.

MEDICAL INSURANCE

Your current insurance may not protect you when traveling. If you are not protected, getting sick on your trip can ruin both your trip and your budget.

Many hospitals might not admit you without a deposit in an emergency, or require you to pay by the time you leave. Generally hospitals in large cities are more apt to take credit cards than those in rural areas, but you should never count on it. You may even need to pay in advance to be airlifted to the appropriate medical facility. Take precautions and get proper insurance before you leave to avoid any possible financial and health catastrophies.

Know about travel insurance, and buy what you need. Be warned that your current health insurance policies may not cover all your needs outside this country, and many plans, including Medicare, do not extend coverage to other countries at all. Usually, insurance money is reimbursed only after a claim has been processed and you are home, but you could need thousands of dollars in cash for medical emergencies while traveling.

For most people this cost would be catastrophic. For a few dollars a day the Frugal Traveler should buy insurance to cover the cost of an accident or illness abroad. There are two types of protection: travelers' health insurance policies and less well-known "Assistance" plans which are designed to provide enough money and assistance quickly to get you through the emergency. Their benefits, costs and services vary. Assistance plans costs depend on the kind of coverage provided, as well as the duration. You can buy them through insurance brokers, travel agents and tour operators, and from assistance service companies. Sometimes they are part of other travel insurance packages. Some credit cards automatically enroll you in an assistance program *free*. Ask!

Travel with your medical history. Carry prescriptions for medication and eyeglasses, as well as extras of both. Get a H.E.L.P. (Help Ensure Life Protection) membership card. On the card is a microfilm insert that contains your medical history, your special medical conditions, and your signature, giving permission to operate in case you're unconscious. The microfilm inserts can be updated once a year, free of charge. Contact H.E.L.P., Box 742505, Houston, TX, 77274-9990.

Tip: In an emergency, go to the largest hospital center in the area. Try to go to a center associated with a university or a teaching hospital.

Tip: Always carry identification including indications of allergies or chronic illnesses and the medications you are taking.

Tip: Check your coverage in your homeowner's policy. If you're traveling on business, check the insurance your company carries. Make sure you are adequately covered. Purchase additional insurance when necessary.

Tip: Be sure to look at the fine print in all insurance policies. For example, some health insurance plans cover any emergency outside the US, others only those within 100 miles of your home or in your state.

In addition to single-trip coverage, many health insurance plans offer coverage for a year, aimed at the frequent traveler. Usually you cannot be outside the country for more than a set period of time. Many policies also have an age limit. Medicare patients interested in supplemental coverage valid outside the US should contact the American Association of Retired Persons Insurance, 800-523-5800 or, in Pennsylvania, 800-492-2024. Be aware as well that coverage might not extend to previous ailments, and you might want to check to see whether the policy limits coverage on—or does not cover—accidents involving high-risk activities such as parachuting, skiing, etc.

Always take insurance claim forms with you. Most US insurance companies require cost itemization, and once home—after you've paid—you might have a hard time getting hospitals or doctors far away to sign forms.

Some types of travel insurance are included in the annual membership fees of some major credit and charge cards, provided you use these cards to buy your tickets. Some travel agencies also supply extensive travel insurance, accident and/or health coverage, during your trip.

You can purchase travel health insurance through most travel agents or you can buy it directly from your insurance company. Some places you may want to check out are: Health Care Abroad, for sickness and accident coverage, is affiliated with 1,000 doctors internationally—call 800-336-3310; International SOS Assistance has a 24-hour hotline worldwide and provides medical evacuation and some health and accident coverage— call 800-523-8930. Other inquiries can be made to Assist Card Corp. of America, 800-221-4564, or Travelers Insurance Companies, 203-277-0111. Travel Guard (800-782-5151) and Access America (800-851-2800) have 24-hour hot lines to provide emergency travel assistance. Travel Guard is endorsed by the American Society of Travel Agents, and Access America, an allied member of the Society, is a subsidiary of Empire Blue Cross and Blue Shield of the National Capital Area. And, as I mentioned before, you can call your own travel agent and insurance agent.

Price comparisons of insurance policies are valid only when comparing which exact features are covered, such as:

- Under what specific circumstances or activities is coverage not valid?
- Who, exactly is covered, and must they be traveling with you?
- When does the coverage begin and end?
- Will any insurance that you already own cover at least part of any travel emergencies?
- Will you get the full benefit of your medical coverage if you have other medical insurance, or will you get only supplementary protection up to the limits allowed?
- Are there any countries where the coverage is not valid?
- What are the limits of the policy?

Get the Latest Information on Immunizations: Information on what is recommended by the Public Health Service of the U.S. Department of Health and Human Services can be found in their annual publication, *Health Information for International Travel,* and their bi-weekly *Blue Sheet* which contains the latest information in vaccination requirements. The nearest office of the U.S. Public Health Service will help you locate a convenient source for the immunization and documentation you'll need. Follow the precautions recommended by your doctor and the Public Health Service.

Vaccinations for some diseases are required by some countries as a condition of entry. If you don't have them, you will either be turned back at immigration or quarantined. Consult the embassy or consulate of the country you'll be visiting to find out the official vaccination and other requirements for entering, and check with your own physician. Vaccination reactions will vary from person to person. Most of these injections can be given right before you travel but some, like typhoid, have to be administered in two stages, two to four weeks apart. Therefore, you should arrange for immunization at least six weeks before your trip. Keeping healthy is part of the Frugal Traveler way to protect your health and your pocketbook.

Some Other Important Health Tips

- When flying, request a seat in the middle of the plane to prevent motion sickness.

- In the sun, use a sun block. Don't ruin your vacation with a severe sunburn.
- When swimming in lakes, streams, rivers and oceans, be careful—many bodies of water carry disease-causing parasites. Check with local health professionals to insure that the water is safe, and swim only where there is a lifeguard.
- Always rub your skin dry with a towel after swimming in unfamiliar waters to remove possible harmful organisms.
- Bring along a good insect repellant for areas of high insect infestation. In case of allergic relations to insect bites, or other allergens, bring along an antihistimine.
- Understand both the personal hygiene and the culture of where you are headed—stock up on toilet paper; toilets in some countries will not have any.
- Bring along medication, even over-the-counter non-prescription drugs, which may not be available in other areas—to settle an upset stomach, for example.
- Air or seasickness: Ask your doctor before you leave home to advise about seasickness and medication for other common travel ailments, diseases, etc.

MEDICAL ATTENTION

If you need medical attention in a foreign country and can't get other help, contact the Tourist Information Office or Tourist Police. Also, the American consulates should have an up-to-date-list of doctors. (To find an English-speaking doctor in any foreign country, ask at your hotel or the US Consulate.)

Before your trip, if you wish, you can get this information from IAMAT (International Association for Medical Assistance to Travelers). For a small donation they furnish a list of English-speaking doctors in 300 foreign cities, plus other very valuable information (call 716-754-5483). For a small fee Intermedic furnishes a list of English-speaking doctors with their qualifications in 200 foreign cities (90 countries) who have agreed to fee ceilings, depending on service provided (call 212-486-8974).

Take advantage of Medic Alert Services, which provide medical identification and information worldwide for travelers—call 800-344-3225.

If you are unsure about where to go for help for any serious injury or illness abroad, contact Overseas Citizens Emergency Center, U.S. State Department, Washington, DC, 202-647-5225. Carry this number with you. This agency will help you contact relatives and quickly transfer emergency funds and medical information.

Know the generic names of the medication you are taking so that you can get it abroad if necessary. Also, if you are under doctor's orders to take a controlled substance, make sure you carry a letter from your doctor explaining your medical needs for such a drug, or you could end up getting arrested.

In a real emergency, look in the front pages of a local telephone book for an emergency number, like the emergency numbers we have in the US.

HELP PREVENT THEFT AND BODILY HARM

If you are going to an out-of-the-way area you should carry your own lock for your hotel rooms. Never put any article of value in the outside pockets of your backpack or attaché case. Attaché cases are among the first targets for thieves—avoid putting valuables in them. Carry most of your money in the form of traveler's checks, and carry your money and passport in a money belt worn inside your clothes. Watch out for your valuables at all times. If your hotel is reputable, use their safe to lock up your valuables.

- Do not go out after dark in unfamiliar areas.
- The loss or theft of traveler's checks or credit cards should be reported at once by cable to the bank or other agency concerned so that payment can be stopped.
- Never let your possessions out of your sight, unless they are secure in the hotel safe or elsewhere.
- Carry only enough money for your immediate requirements.
- Change money only at a bank or other reliable source such as a reputable hotel or department store. Banks are often, but not always, the best places to exchange currency. Banks may charge commissions that hotels and stores do not. Many major hotels and stores use the banks' posted

exchange rates. Take nothing for granted—compare rates in two or three places before cashing a substantial amount of money. Try to avoid airport banks or exchange desks with their captive-audience rates, as well as smaller shops, where you can expect to pay a premium.

In many places you'll get a better rate of exchange if your dollars are in traveler's checks, and a credit card can make money for you. It will allow unused cash to earn interest in the bank until the bills arrive, which may not be for several months. My personal advice is that for maximum security and detailed expense records, for your boss and the I.R.S., use a credit card whenever you can.

When leaving your hotel room, turn on the radio or TV, put on a light, take valuables with you, put out a Do Not Disturb sign, lock your room and keep your key with you. Before retiring, lock the doors and windows securely, using chains and dead bolts.

LOST PASSPORTS

If you lose your passport or if it is stolen, report it immediately to the local police and the U.S. Passport Office in Washington, DC. In foreign countries, report it to any US consulate office, and a US embassy can replace it.

VISAS

Passports are usually required to obtain visas, and it may take four to six weeks to get one. Travelers should check either the consulate or the embassy at their destination to determine what documents are required to obtain them. This information is also printed in a publication called *Visa Requirements of Foreign Governments,* which is available by sending a self-addressed, stamped envelope to the Bureau of Consular Affairs, CA/PA Room 5807, Department of State, Washington, DC 20520. But also get in touch with the embassy or consulate of the country you are planning to visit to make sure the information has not been superseded. In emergencies, it may be very costly to extend a visa in some countries, so take maximum visa time, just in case your exit from a country must be unexpectedly delayed.

Very Important: Leave your itinerary for friends and relatives to be able to reach you. You may not be able to imagine why they would need to, but, as the Frugal Traveler knows, it never hurts to be prepared!

IT'S UP TO YOU TO TAKE PRECAUTIONS

When it comes to travel problems and emergencies Frugal Travelers live by the maxim "an ounce of prevention is worth a pound of cure." Indeed, Frugal Travelers, you are now more knowledgeable in preventing and dealing with potentially very costly and perhaps devastatingly harmful catastrophies related to travel experience.

▪ 9 ▪

Checklists for the

Prepared Traveler

CHECK YOUR HOME

Review your insurance policies to make sure that your home and its contents, as well as any possessions you are taking or leaving, are adequately covered. Check on medical insurance to make sure that you and traveling family members are adequately covered and that coverage extends to all geographic areas on your itinerary. Check and see if you need specific travel insurance and car insurance in addition to what you already have. The following are some things to do before you leave.

☑ Make sure all legal documents are up to date—wills, etc.

☑ Make sure all your insurance premiums and other important bills are paid through the date of your return.

- ☑ Make sure burglar and fire alarms are working.
- ☑ Put your house on the police "dark house" list.
- ☑ Set lighting inside your home to work on set automatic timers.
- ☑ Secure all doors and windows.
- ☑ Depending on the season, ask someone to remove snow or cut the lawn.
- ☑ Stop mail, newspaper, and milk deliveries.
- ☑ Bring pets to a kennel or to whoever will care for them.
- ☑ Water plants, or bring them to whoever will care for them.
- ☑ Turn off or lower hot water temperature.
- ☑ Leave itinerary with friend or relative in case you have to be reached.
- ☑ Put valuables in safety deposit box (do not take valuables with you that you do not really need to take).
- ☑ Turn down (or up) settings on thermostat.
- ☑ Disconnect electrical appliances.
- ☑ Room by room, check to see that each door and window is locked, and look for anything left behind.
- ☑ Double-check that you have taken all important travel items for your carry-on luggage—hotel reservation numbers, traveler's checks, cash and credit cards, passports, tickets, and keys to your house.
- ☑ Lock door as you leave. Make sure it is shut *and* locked.

MISCELLANEOUS CHECKLIST ITEMS
FOR ALL TRAVELERS TO TAKE

☑ Any special medical records and identifications like alert bracelets, etc.

☑ Prescription drugs

☑ Sun and eyeglasses

☑ Aspirin, Band-Aids, and other nonprescription drugs you can anticipate you might need

☑ Your own smoke detector, in case the hotel's is not working

☑ Hairbrush and comb

☑ Toothbrush and paste

☑ Cosmetics

☑ Razor

☑ Deodorant

☑ Shampoo, soap

☑ Manicure set

☑ Sun block or lotion

☑ Skin moisturizer and cream

☑ Tissues

☑ Thermometer

☑ Accessories and essential jewelry

☑ Sewing kit

☑ Plastic bags

☑ Comfortable shoes

☑ Jacket/coverup/rain gear

☑ Maps

☑ Insurance claim forms

AUTOMOBILE CHECKLIST

☑ Registration and license (plus International License, if traveling where needed)

☑ Proof of insurance

☑ Auto Club identification (if applicable)

☑ Flashlight, extra batteries

☑ Oil company credit cards

☑ Extra set of car keys

☑ First-aid kit

☑ Plastic bags and paper bags

☑ Paper towels

☑ Emergency flares

☑ Sunglasses/extra set of prescription glasses

☑ Large water container

☑ Tool kit

☑ Blanket

☑ Check spare tire

☑ Important telephone numbers

☑ Make sure car is serviced before any long trip (see service chart)

☑ Maps

RECORD OF INSURANCE POLICIES

Make sure policy premiums are paid up to date, and that they cover you and all travelers throughout the time you are away and in all the areas of your itinerary.

Kind of
Insurance _____ Amount _____

Agent's Name _____ Telephone Number _____

Company Name _____ Telephone Number _____

Address: _____ Policy Number _____

Exp. Date _____ Premium_____

Notes:

_____

Kind of
Insurance _____ Amount _____

Agent's Name _____ Telephone Number _____

Company Name _____ Telephone Number _____

Address: _____ Policy Number _____

Exp. Date _____ Premium_____

Notes:

_____

Kind of
Insurance _____ Amount _____

Agent's Name _____ Telephone Number _____

Company Name _____ Telephone Number _____

Address: _____ Policy Number _____

Exp. Date _____ Premium_____

CREDIT CARD RECORDS—TAKE THIS WITH YOU AND LEAVE A COPY HOME.

Emergency Card
Card Name _____Loss Tel #_____
Card Issuer _____ Address _____
Card Number _____ Exp. Date _____

Emergency Card
Card Name _____Loss Tel #_____
Card Issuer _____ Address _____
Card Number _____ Exp. Date _____

Emergency Card
Card Name _____Loss Tel #_____
Card Issuer _____ Address _____
Card Number _____ Exp. Date _____

Emergency Card
Card Name _____Loss Tel #_____
Card Issuer _____ Address _____
Card Number _____ Exp. Date _____

Emergency Card
Card Name _____Loss Tel #_____
Card Issuer _____ Address _____
Card Number _____ Exp. Date _____

TRAVELER'S CHECK RECORD

Emergency Card
Name _____Loss Tel #_____
Check Issuer _____ Address _____
Check Number _____ Exp. Date _____

Emergency Card
Name _____Loss Tel #_____
Check Issuer _____ Address _____
Check Number _____ Exp. Date _____

IMPORTANT PHONE NUMBERS
TO TAKE WITH YOU

Names and Addresses   **Telephone**

Doctors

Vet.

Insurance Agents

Neighbors

Relatives

_____
_____
_____
_____
_____
_____

EXPENSE SUMMARY
(FOR INTERNAL REVENUE SERVICE
AND EMPLOYER)

Date	Meals	Transpor-tation	Phone	Enter-tainment	Purpose (Who, What Where)	Misc.	Daily total

• 10 •

Bon Voyage!

Well, Frugal Travelers, we've discussed everything from how to get an airplane ticket at bargain prices, to where and when to go to save the most money and what to do if you find yourself in Istanbul, or anywhere else, without your passport. We've talked about the general ideas the Frugal Traveler uses to plan a vacation and the specific tactics that will save the most time and money. We've talked about the importance of planning ahead and how to deal with surprises no amount of planning could have foreseen. Now, I think, it's time to set out and journey into the dreamy blue yonder of the traveler's paradise. Remember, as you travel on your trip,

Bon Voyage!

and through life, A$k and then A¢t. As a Frugal Traveler, all your decisions should be considered according to the value you place on your time, yourself and your money.

Have a safe and pleasant trip!

Bon Voyage!

Marion Joyce

P.S. Drop me a postcard if you have any questions or travel suggestions, and tell me how you enjoyed your trip! Write to me at POB 116, Tuckahoe, New York 10707.

P.S.S. And don't forget to use the money-saving coupons at the back of this book!

If you enjoyed this book, you'll also want to order *The Frugal Shopper*

Learn how to save money, get cash refunds or pay nothing for almost everything you buy. Over 50 valuable coupons included.

And you can also order extra copies of this book, *The Frugal Traveler,* for friends, relatives, frequent travelers everywhere, or for yourself, for the extra coupons.

For your convenience, use the coupon to order. Attach an additional page if necessary. These books are also available at your local bookstore or wherever paperback books are sold.

G.P. Putnam's Sons, 390 Murray Hill Parkway, Dept. B, East Rutherford, N.J. 07073.

Please send me _____ copies of *The Frugal Shopper* (SBN 399-51278-0) at $6.95 each.
Please send _____ copies of *The Frugal Traveler* (SBN 399-51409-0) at $6.95 each.

Enclosed is my ☐ check ☐ money order. Subtotal $_____
Please charge my ☐ Visa ☐ MasterCard. Postage &

Card # _____   Handling $___1.50

Expiration date _____

                                    Sales Tax $_____

Name _____ Total $_____

Address _____

City _____State _____ Zip _____

Signature as on charge card _____

Please allow 4 to 6 weeks for delivery.

CUT HERE.

CAPTAIN'S CORNER

0-DUVAL ST.   KEY WEST, FL 33040
Ocean Key House Watersports
305-296-8865

SAVE
SEE REVERSE SIDE FOR DETAILS

10%   **SAVE**   **10%**

The Sunshine Airline

Save 10% on travel any Tuesday, Wednesday, Thursday
booked at least 7 days in advance.
Valid November 1, 1987 through January 15, 1989

Call 1-800-423-0535 for reservations and you must mention
FRUGAL TRAVEL PROGRAM to get savings

CUT HERE.

FREE...
THREE DAYS
OF
CARIBBEAN
SAILING

This offer is available
with any seven day
charter during the
period May 15 through
November 15
Call toll free -
1-800-225-2520
or inside Massachusetts
(617) 599-7990

CUT HERE.

THESE COUPONS ARE REDEEMABLE. CLIP AND SAVE!

✂ CUT HERE.

✂ CUT HERE.

✂ CUT HERE.

THESE COUPONS ARE REDEEMABLE. CLIP AND SAVE!

Professionally written and produced tour tapes point out all the sights so you don't miss a thing.

THESE COUPONS ARE REDEEMABLE. CLIP AND SAVE!

THESE COUPONS ARE REDEEMABLE. CLIP AND SAVE!

SAVE 20%

Present this coupon upon check-in and receive a 20% savings on the current prevailing rate. This offer is good for your entire stay.

Advance reservations are recommended. For reservations call the properties direct or use the toll-free number. This coupon cannot be used in conjunction with other discounts or special rates.

FOR TOLL FREE RESERVATIONS
PhiSTAR (800) 854-6111

CUT HERE.

Firestone

America's Home For Car Service

CUT HERE.

Firestone

America's Home For Car Service

CUT HERE.

Firestone

America's Home For Car Service

Firestone

America's Home For Car Service

Firestone

America's Home For Car Service

THESE COUPONS ARE REDEEMABLE. CLIP AND SAVE!

Become a seasoned traveler with the Living Language Video series which offers instruction in French, Spanish or German. These videos place you in practical situations, such as a hotel, restaurant, shopping, etc., while allowing you to learn at your own pace. Use this coupon for a 10% discount.

THESE COUPONS ARE REDEEMABLE. CLIP AND SAVE!

CUT HERE.

CUT HERE.

CUT HERE.

THESE COUPONS ARE REDEEMABLE. CLIP AND SAVE!

THESE COUPONS ARE REDEEMABLE. CLIP AND SAVE!

THESE COUPONS ARE REDEEMABLE. CLIP AND SAVE!

THESE COUPONS ARE REDEEMABLE. CLIP AND SAVE!

Steve Colgate's
ffshore Sailing School Ltd.

INVITES YOU TO LEARN TO SAIL AND SAVE 10% ON TUITION. PICK THE LOCATION THAT'S BEST FOR YOU. CAPE COD, NEW YORK, THE HAMPTONS, FLORIDA, OR TORTOLA IN THE BRITISH VIRGIN ISLANDS.

**SAVE
10%**

**CALL FOR DETAILS
212-885-3200
800-221-4326 OUTSIDE NY**

**SAVE
10%**

✂ CUT HERE.

Club Express Membership Application

Name

Company Name

Address

City/State/Zip

American Express Card Number   Expiration Date

Signature

Mail application to:
Stouffer Hotels Club Express
29800 Bainbridge Road, Solon, Ohio 44139

**STOUFFER HOTELS
CLUB EXPRESS**

✂ CUT HERE.

Enjoy an **upgrade** from a regular room to a Club Floor room, suite or best available room. Present the adjacent upgrade coupons at time of check-in. Offer based on space availability.

Call toll-free 1-800-HOTELS-1

Please show your savings card when you check-in and retain the card for future travel. Offer expires Dec. 31, 1989. Not valid in conjunction with any other offer.

 Offer good for one upgrade presented at check-in expires Dec. 31, 1989

 Offer good for one upgrade presented at check-in expires Dec. 31, 1989

 Offer good for one upgrade presented at check-in expires Dec. 31, 1989

 Offer good for one upgrade presented at check-in expires Dec. 31, 1989

✂ CUT HERE.

CUT HERE. ✂

SAVE 10%

RENT A FORD OR OTHER FINE CAR FROM

$69. 00
PER
WEEK

PRESENT THIS AD FOR

10% DISCOUNT AT TIME
OF RENTAL

OFF REGULAR RENTAL RATE

NOT VALID WITH 69.00 SPECIAL OR ANY
OTHER DISCOUNT OFFER--EXPIRES 12-31-89

RENT-A-CAR
SEE REVERSE FOR LOCATIONS

CUT HERE. ✂

SAVE 15%

RENT A FORD OR OTHER FINE CAR FROM

$69. 00
PER
WEEK

PRESENT THIS AD FOR

15% DISCOUNT AT TIME
ON SECOND RENTAL OF RENTAL

OFF REGULAR RENTAL RATE

NOT VALID WITH 69.00 SPECIAL OR ANY
OTHER DISCOUNT OFFER--EXPIRES 12-31-89

RENT-A-CAR
SEE REVERSE FOR LOCATIONS

CUT HERE. CUT HERE. CUT HERE.

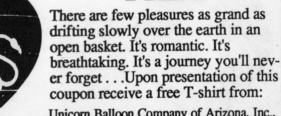